#WDF
The Naked Truth
{The Story of My 20-Year, Bipolar, Biracial Marriage}

Timna, LLC
2017

Copyright © 2017 by Timna Augustine

All rights reserved. This book or any portion thereof may not be reproduced or used in any manner whatsoever without the express written permission of the publisher except for the use of brief quotations in a book review or scholarly journal.

First Printing: 2017

Edited by: Michele Kendall/A Dream Realized

ISBN: 978-1-387-16694-7

Timna, LLC
Atlanta, GA 30319

www.Timna.com

Ordering Information:

Special discounts are available on quantity purchases by corporations, associations, educators, and others. For details, contact Timna@Timna.com

U.S. Trade bookstores and wholesalers:

Please contact Timna@Timna.com

Acknowledgements

Many thanks to my family for giving me the space and time to write! You guys are awesome! You ROCK!

Also many shout outs to my extended family, friends, and my social network! You guys are the BOMB! For you Millennials, I just used an old school word.

Oh, I don't want to forget to say thank you to the many readers of this book! I love you for investing your hard earn money on WDF and on me. I hope you say What Da F*ck?! (WDF?!) When you read this book. Don't forget to make sure you tell a friend to buy a copy.

My mom always told me when I was growing up that…

"Birds of a Feather Flock Together"

So let the story of my 20 year marriage enlighten you… and if you're a part my flock, you ROCK!

Introduction

Thank you for taking the leap of faith in joining me on this journey of my bipolar, biracial relationship.

Who am I? Not a writer! Just an inspiring, speaker, philosopher, comedian, and teacher! I was born in Brooklyn, NY in 1974. I'm a first generation American. My parents are immigrants from Central America, Costa Rica, and Panama. Therefore, I consider myself Afro-Latina.

Growing up in NYC allowed me to be culturally diverse. My parents integrated our Anglo-Saxon neighborhood when I was five. Our family was one of the first black families to purchase a home in an all White neighborhood in the early 1980s. By 1989 the community completely changed and was integrated with many Afro-Caribbean families. My brother and I were raised to be Caribbean American. However, we went to culturally diverse schools in NYC. I lived my life embracing people from all walks of life. My parents instilled confidence, loyalty, religion and hard working values in both my brother and I. These values allowed me to be outspoken and a builder of my dreams. The Latina, side of me allowed me to become a lover of love.

In 1989, we moved to Tampa, Florida because I was a reckless teenager in love. They thought moving me to a rural area of Tampa would distance me from my boyfriend and prevent me from getting pregnant. I was upset at the time, but now, I know this was the best thing that they could have done for me because this transition helped me to see another way of life and to get out of my comfort zone.

So how did I get here?! Twenty years of marriage and writing a book about the NAKED TRUTH of my relationship. I'm still scratching my head about this. All I can tell you is that when you start writing, you never know what will come out of it (smile). For me, when I completed each chapter of this book, I said, WDF?! and you will too.

CONTENTS

Chapter 1
The Beginning

Chapter 2
The Trophy

Chapter 3
The Reality Check

Chapter 4
Who Are Those Strangers?

Chapter 5
Breathe

Chapter 6
The Arrival

Chapter 7
The Longest Year of My Life

Chapter 8
The Never Ending Sickness

Chapter 9
Champagne Anyone

Chapter 10
The Big Move

Chapter 11
The Storm

Chapter 12
The Problem with Texting

Chapter 13
Volcano

Chapter 14
4 Weeks of Clarity

Never say never

Chapter 1:
The Beginning

Love is in the eyes of the beholder

Yes. What Da F*ck?! is the theme of my story. You will say these words many times as you read this book. The story of my 20-year relationship with my husband, Mr. Swiss, is captivating, with cultural differences fast-paced movement, and a whirlwind of emotions.

One day after our 19th anniversary, I asked myself What Da F*ck?! How did we get here? I wondered what the secret to being married until death do us part was. I wondered what the naked truth of my relationship was.

So, I started to write and, in doing so, my world shifted; the words that follow reveal the roller coaster of emotions and expose the hidden deep dark wounds within my marriage. At times, I laughed, I cried, and then I said, *"What Da F*ck?! How did we get here? How did we become so stupid in this relationship?"* Then, the question came to me. Should I stay or should I leave?

The Beginning of the Perfect Relationship

In 1996, I was 23, a new graduated of Clark Atlanta University, completely in my comfort zone back home with my parents until I was ready to go back to Atlanta to earn my Master's Degree. I wasn't looking to change and wanted to remain happy in my ignorance!

Like many of us experience early in dating life, currently, or will perhaps in the future, I had relationship issues. I wanted to be with a man, who loved me for me and respected me. However, for some reason, I liked men who used me emotionally, lied to me, and cheated on me.

The men that I was interested in were 6 feet or taller, chocolate brown, athletic, with lots of swag (high self-esteem), had high earning potentials, great attitude, and could dig Caribbean music, tall, dark and handsome. Isn't this what every woman wants and desires? Research has shown that there are only 3.9% of these guys out there! Really what were the chances of me finding a guy that has it all? Let's face it, slim to none.

I had no idea that the image of the man that I eventually married would not represent my black knight in shining armor.

I was a blissfully ignorant young girl, eager to fall in love. I was an adamant, dominant, loving, playful, spontaneous person. So, why not me? Why was I not getting what I wanted? Why was I failing in the matchmaking business? I wanted to be like my parents, married and in a long-term relationship. What happened to me? Why couldn't I find someone? The number one word to me at this time was, stability.

"Stability: being in a relationship not dating around like a slut..." as my mom once called me because I was dating a few guys at the same time. In college, I dated three guys at the same time, because I was looking for Mr. Right. I was like Princess Charming trying the same shoe on different guys. I asked myself, "Am I a slut or am I just like any average girl looking for love?"

My Floridian

Mr. Florida, I swore, was the ONE when he entered my life. Charming and cultured, he was a tall chocolate dream with an amazing athletic body, holding down a great marketing and sales job. He also had a side gig modeling. He was artistic in nature and spontaneous. He was the best swimmer, the best hunter, the best fisherman, the best, in fact, at everything. Yes, Mr. Florida was the kind of man you could bring home to your parents. But, he was a bit mysterious. Mr. Florida kept a secret, one that would eventually cause our break up. Mr. Florida, oh Mr. Florida, why did you lie?

My Californian

Mr. California, was a walking piece of art. He assembled every item of clothing he worn as if he was perfecting a sculpture. The man even air dried his jeans. More than physical beauty, Mr. California was wise. His mystery, his eccentricity, and his Afrocentricity all drew me to him. His romance also charmed me. Sometimes we talked all night and cuddled. One night after I walked into his apartment, he surprised me with a rose petal bath, hot and ready for me to get in. I relaxed while he prepared dinner. He was that guy who knew what to say and when to say it. A great listener, Mr. California shared his deep thoughts with me. We were great friends and lovers.

However, (there was always a however), his romance couldn't compete with one huge problem: his phobia of kissing. How can anyone be in a long-term relationship without kissing? Was he hiding something? Maybe it was the vulnerability or an inability to give himself entirely, but I wasn't going to wait to have my heartbroken. I decided to trust my intuition. Could I live without passionate kissing? Umm No!

My New Yorker

Mr. New York, my tall, dark, and sexy New Yorker, dripped confidence. He had the kind of New York swag that shouted pure self-assurance. One step into a room and heads turned. He commanded his audience with just a look. His voice made me smile every time we spoke. I felt protected around him. And yet, something was missing: trust. He didn't trust me, and I didn't trust him. We played a regular tug-of-war game with our trust for one another. We never argued, but we knew we couldn't be together because neither of us wanted to submit to the other. We had our guards up at all times. We didn't fully trust or fully commit to one another. We silently always knew that we belonged to someone else.

One night on one of my many trips to New York, we stood in front of his building, the street lights glaring at our eyes. We looked at each other and knew we had to decide between a life together and a life apart. His choice was not me. He had another girlfriend at his college that he loved. I looked at Mr. New York with tears in my eyes. I was not the one and I surely didn't want to be the second best of anything. We embraced knowing that this was our last kiss, the final hurrah. The death of our relationship made our last kiss the most passionate kiss I ever had. We both teared up and walked away. He watched me get in my white Dodge Colt, and I watched him enter his building. I drove away feeling lost.

Would I find love? Would I ever be someone's Number 1?

Blinded By Expectation

These three guys had one thing in common: they were not ready to commit to me fully. I was trying to make the shoe fit, but it never fit. None of the guys was my perfect match. I needed an online dating site, but that didn't exist in the late 90s. Maybe, I needed a dating coach, but I couldn't afford one. Perhaps, I just needed a reality check.

Maybe I was dating multiple guys, because I wasn't ready to commit. They felt my unfocused energy and my lack of investment in the relationship. I thought I was ready but was I? I was a hot mess!

Later on that summer...

My parents knew my pain. They knew that their bold, funny, and smart daughter desired to find a real match.

One day, a young man, a traveler from a distant land (Switzerland), was seeking something different: a car. He came off the bus and stopped in front of my father's small lot that held approximately fifteen used cars. The lot was dusty, little specks of grass separated one car from another, all bunched up on this small lot. Something about this car lot drew Mr. Swiss' eyes; maybe it was the guy standing in front of the lot with his arms open welcoming people who entered the used car lot. Mr. Swiss, walked onto the lot and this man, my father opened his arms and said, *"This is your lucky day!"* Oh, I wonder what was going on in Mr. Swiss's mind, and I also wonder if my father knew that it really was this young man's lucky day.

At the time, Mr. Swiss spoke little English. He only understood what my dad's smile meant: kindness.

Mr. Swiss, purchased a Black 1986 Nissan Pulsar from my father. He then befriended my father's Jamaican salesman who happened to love the sport of his profession: soccer. Mr. Swiss admired the culture and loved the attention he received from the Jamaican and my father. They welcomed him and treated him well. He was even invited to rent a room in the home of my parents' best friend. He trained each day on the soccer field, drove his new car, lived in a home with a loving older couple, and made new friends.

Soon after, my mother said to me (in her Caribbean accent), *"Timna, there's this guy at your father's car lot that comes and hangs out. He purchased a car from your father and he is new to this country. So, why don't you show him around?"*

I was immediately apprehensive!

I didn't care or want to know anything about this guy from Switzerland. A man from Europe was the last thing on my mind. He is a White European that doesn't speak English. What would I do with him? I can't even communicate with him. Hanging out with him will be a waste of my time! Plus, he is White!

I told my mother, *"I do NOT want to show him around! I don't know him! He's a stranger! What do you think I am, a tour guide? I don't think so!"*

My mother told me to behave and stop being mean and ignorant, and, quite frankly, bratty. She told me to *"add some cream to my coffee."* I started to laugh and said, *"Why am I adding cream to this beautiful black coffee? I just graduated from a historically Black university. So, why would I want to entertain a White stranger? Excuse me!"*

I decided to ignore her request. I would never date a White guy.

Never say never!

A few weeks passed and I decided to go to my father's car business. I walked in and noticed this young man, Mr. Swiss, sitting in the office at the desk, watching the shop while my father went for a lunch break. He looked like a terrorist with a wild beard, short black hair and small hazel eyes that seemed to hide behind all of that facial hair. He needed a shave. He was also wearing cutoff shorts with a dark green fanny pack that crossed his waist. He had hairy, strong thick legs and he was wearing flat blue slip on sneakers with no laces. I used to call these types of sneakers Italian shoes. When I usually look at guys, I would decide if I was attracted to them. I was definitely not attracted to this guy. One glance at him and I knew he was not my type. He was White and hairy. These were the two big negatives for me. My parents are crazy. I would never date a guy like him. What did they find attractive in him and why would I even hang out with this person?

"Where is my father?" He sat there like a deer in headlights giving no response. Pulling out a small pocket dictionary, he searched for the translation of my words. Something clicked in my head. He really didn't speak English. How cute. Suddenly, he started to look cute. Maybe it was the accent. But he still wasn't cute enough for me. He was a not only a stranger, but strange to me.

I decided to start a conversation with him because I wanted to prove to my mother that she was wrong. I didn't need any cream in my coffee. Plus, I was bored and wanted some entertainment, so I started a conversation with this European and his dictionary.

Me: *Hey, so what are you doing out here?*
Mr. Swiss: *What am I doing out here?*
Me: *Yes, what made you come to America?*
Mr. Swiss: *I come to America to play Football.*
Me: *Football*
Mr. Swiss: looking at his dictionary... *Sooooccccerr*
Me: *Oh, Soccer.*
Mr. Swiss: *Yes, Soccer.*
Me: *So what else?*
Mr. Swiss: *I left my country to play soccer.*
Me: *You left your country to play soccer?*

While he was looking for every word in the dictionary, I became more curious about this guy. It was interesting to talk with someone who had no idea what you are saying. I was thoroughly amused; I started to laugh and smile about his lack of knowledge of the English language! I started to realize that I was girlishly happy around him. Hmmm, maybe, it was the accent!

Even though he didn't speak English. Wow! He actually seems like a great guy. I think we can hang out.

My father was running errands and decided not to return from his lunch break because I was now there. So an hour passed, then a second hour passed. This European and I laughed, talked, and flirted. He asked questions and I, of course, answered all of them. After several hours, my father returned. We decided to take a leap of faith and continue hanging out. Actually, I asked him to go to the movies with me because I was bored.

He had no idea what he would be doing at the movies because he couldn't understand the language. Plus, how was he supposed to use his dictionary in the dark when the movie was playing. Oh well, he decided to come along because, I convinced him. How could he pass up an opportunity to hang out with me? I had no idea what this day would bring or the adventure that we would have.

I jumped into the Nissan Pulsar he bought from my dad and drove off into the unknown.

First, we toured two soccer fields where he played and he introduced me to his fellow teammates. I was sure they had a puzzled looks on their faces. I knew I was not what they expected. I was 112 pound 5'5 brown skin girl with short natural hair who looked like she was fifteen. I was not the image that they thought he would be out on a date with. Trust me, if I was them, I would've thought the same thing. In fact, I thought the same thing.

The conversation was good, so our lunch date was longer than expected. After lunch, we went to our original destination, the movies. We saw Thinner by Stephen King. It was a 1996 horror film about a guy who commits a crime and is then cursed by the father of the victim to become thinner and thinner until he dies. He was an obese man who just got thinner and thinner. This movie was a thriller so it was definitely hard for Mr. Swiss to keep up and hard for me to translate. This movie was the longest most, disturbing movie I've ever seen with an individual. He didn't understand the movie at all. Plus, I tried to explain but it was difficult to explain to a person who spoke another language. He was lost in translation and I was tickled pink. We both were so just happy to be around each other! Maybe it was just our synergy. The Universe wanted us to be together.

We left the movie theater, and despite our synergy, I felt like everyone was looking at me. I thought I was on stage because I was walking with this White stranger in the mall. I spent the whole time worrying that another Black person would comment. Of course, someone did.

An African-American guy was walking with his friends. He was the leader of the pack who needed attention. He screamed out to me after passing us, "What are you doing with him?" I looked at him and screamed back, "What? What did you say?" He said," Why are you with that guy and not with a brother?" Then, I said, "Excuse me. Who cares who I'm with? What is your f*cking problem?" The guy said, "You're with him when there are some great guys right here!" So, I said, "Are you taking me to the movies and paying for my ticket?"

This guy and I continued our small argument and Mr. Swiss was shocked. He wondered what was going on and was wondering if everything was okay. I felt his panic and fear so I stopped.

I just stopped arguing with this young guy and walked away.

I knew immediately that I attracted that mess because I was looking for it. I attracted this negative attention because I was focused on it. I was so nervous about what someone thought or would say about me walking with this White guy that my fear and my thoughts became my reality.

Who cares about whom I'm walking around with? I did. I cared about the impression that I was leaving on people's minds and what they thought about me and my choice of company. I felt everyone was looking and peering in my window criticizing me and judging me on my choice of the person that I liked and would eventually love. The fear of judgment was a real problem for me and I knew it.

We left the mall and the date continued…

We walked on the beach, we took a stroll on the breeze way and then he said, *"I will marry my next girlfriend."*

What? I panicked. Wait a minute!

My mind was flooded.

We just met a few hours ago!
Is this guy crazy?
This feels great I like him. BUT, what the heck did he just say?
This is too much for me to handle.
Is he crazy?
What is he saying?
He doesn't even speak English!

Thoughts flooded my mind like waves on the ocean, slapping my body in the water with no control. I felt like I was about to drown with no life preserver. This information was overwhelming. Yet, for some reason, I found comfort in his commitment to his next girlfriend, which could be me. While it was the comfort that I was looking for, I felt very confused and stressed by his appearance and who he was. Many thoughts raced through my mind, flooding my brain.

Is he the one? But he doesn't look like the one; he doesn't smell like the one. He doesn't speak my language. He can't be the one!?

The 12 hour Date Continued

We went to dinner at Bennigan's for about two hours or more. I took time to talk to him and answer questions he had about America, the Caribbean culture, and my experience at my university. I asked him questions about where he was from, his cultural background, and our differences. He was from a small village where there was one school building for all the village kids. He had a business which he sold to come to America to fulfill his passion of being a professional soccer player.

We also talked about the argument that I had with the guy earlier in the mall. As the night went on and the questions became deeper, he made me think. Why had I been arguing with those guys? What was the point?

It was midnight and I knew my parents would begin to worry. Remember there were no cell phones back then. So I told him to take me home. We drove up to my home and we sat just to finish a last bit of our conversation. Then he leaned over, placed both of his hands gently on my cheeks, and asked me for a kiss. I was shocked and nervous all at the same time.

No one has ever asked me for a kiss, especially in this way. Of course I said yes. Of course, my parents were standing at the door waiting for me. The kiss was soft and sweet with no tongue. Just a soft sweet kiss on the lips that seemed to last for minutes. It was so romantic. But I panicked! I ran in the house and screamed, *"I just kissed a White guy!"* What the Hell!

That kiss was strangely good!

My parents looked at me and asked, *"Are you okay?"* I said, *"Yes. I need to call my friends so, I will talk to you guys later."*

I ran upstairs to my room, which was still decorated in the decor of my youth. I felt like I was in Junior High again, nervous and ready to tell my friends about my first kiss with a White guy. So, I called my friend and screamed, *"I just kissed a White guy!"* And she replied, *"So? Why are you calling me at midnight?"*

Then I called another, and she said, *"Great Timna."* Then I called another, and she said, *"Okay Timna."* Then, I called another and she was like, *"What is wrong with you Timna? No one cares if he is White. It's late."* After the 5th girlfriend, I realized no one cares if he is White! No one cares but me. So what! Why am I freaking out about this? Why do I care so much about what others think?

Why was I so stressed about kissing a White guy?

I had no idea why? Maybe, because he was outside of my comfort zone! Maybe because I programmed myself to only have eyes for a brown skin man.

My Comfort Zone:

I couldn't sleep all night, I had questions running through my head. What are people going to say about me? What are they going to think about me? What are my friends truly thinking? Am I a sellout?

I was so confused about the whole situation! I called my friends again in the morning for approval, and they thought I was crazy to even question my situation. They blew me off or just let me ramble about the date and my experience. Not one of them was concerned about who I dated. They were just happy that I was happy.

It was still odd to me, I was outside of my comfort zone and afraid to leave. Throughout college, I was only around Black people; I was attracted to only Black men, and I saw myself having children that represented my culture and with whom I identified. I loved myself and I didn't want to be challenged or questioned about loving someone else that didn't represent my Black beauty.

My comfort zone was the brown skin guy that was over six feet tall, with an athletic body, who spoke the same language and who represented my ideal mate. The guy that would fit the glass slipper that I made for him. I realized that because I couldn't sleep or eat, I was in love. I was uncomfortable but, comfortable being in love with someone who was not my ideal image of a boyfriend.

That morning after calling all of my friends, I asked myself "What do you have to lose?" The answer was, nothing. I had already dated three guys who represented my ideal but were not the perfect match. So, what did I have to lose? Nothing! But I had a lot to gain, the exploration of something new.

WDF?!
It's now time to Live
Life 4 Real

Chapter 2:
The Trophy

You can only win a trophy if you play in the game

At the beginning of my love story, I had to take a leap of faith, to be vulnerable, to think outside the box, explore, conquer fears, and commit to the adventure of Living Life 4 Real. Not worrying about what others may think or say but, honestly Living Life 4 Real for me! My feelings, my desires and my vision of my future was already written. Now it was my job to follow my intuitions and path.

I was writing my story, my reality TV show! I was one of the main characters, and the writers were us!

The first three months blew by fast; we spent every waking hour together. When Mr. Swiss woke up, he called me, just to say good morning. Sometimes he was even at my parents' front door ringing the doorbell as they prepared to go to work.

He was ready for school because I was his teacher and he was my student. He was eager to learn more about me and to become more proficient in the English language. I was the patient teacher willing to know more about my student and assist him in any way to be proficient in English. This relationship was a full-time job. Getting to know one another took time and effort. We talked and talked all day long. We asked each other questions; we translated using a dictionary, we watched TV and educated each other on our cultural differences. We took the time to explain answers by using gestures, objects, and we explored. I also accompanied him to all of his games. We were like glue.

The Questions

The questions that Mr. Swiss asked me were funny and exciting. The number one question that stood out was about the way my skin, smelled and felt. After being in the pool one day swimming, he asked me, *"Why doesn't your towel get soaking wet like mine?"* Well, that was an interesting question. My towel never gets wet. Then I noticed that the water seemed to stay on his skin while it pearled off of mine. The water didn't settle on my skin; it just ran down. When I put the towel on my skin, and it touches it, there is little to no moisture compared to his because the water had already dropped off. Whereas his skin the water seemed to lay there waiting to be wiped off. Therefore, the towel was soaking up most of the water off of his skin compared to mine. This conversation would've never taken place if I hadn't taken a leap of faith out of my comfort zone.

The Conversation

Mr. Swiss asked me in his broken English, *"Timna, why don't your skin smell? I thought it would smell bad."* What the hell? What kind of question is that? I said, *"That's an interesting question. Why would you assume my skin would smell bad or have an odor?"*

Mr. Swiss told me, *"I met an African lady in Switzerland, who had chocolate skin like yours and she also had an exotic look. I was attracted to her. We had a connection but, when we were touching, I noticed that her skin had a bad smell. This smell was a turnoff for me. I couldn't continue to be with her. It was not a scent that I liked."* While laughing, I said, *"I assume that you thought that all brown women have this distinct smell."* Mr. Swiss asked, *"Why are you laughing?"*

I told him, *"Some cultures or people that look like me use different perfumes or lotions that place an odor or different scent on their skin. This scent is ideal for their environment. However, this scent may not be great for others outside of their cultural group. I, on the other hand, love, soft smells and I don't like aggressive smells like Cocoa Butter or Organic Shea Butters without added perfumes. These oils are perfect for brown skin but can be unique in the scent that it carries."*

My big question for him was, *"Since we're talking about smells, why don't you wear deodorant?"* Mr. Swiss had a look of fear on his face, and you could see the wonder run across his forehead. He was baffled at my line of questioning. He had no clue that he needed to wear deodorant. I continued, "*We're in Florida and it's hot. You can sometimes have a manly scent, and it's not pleasing to my nose as the African lady didn't have a pleasing scent to you.*" Mr. Swiss wanted to know, "*Do I smell?*" He didn't say much, but the puzzled look on his face told me that he truly didn't realize that not wearing deodorant would be a problem.

WOW, he had no clue about the issue of not using deodorant. His lack of knowledge regarding his odor was so baffling to me. I sat there wondering how I could communicate this to him without offending him. I asked, "*Didn't you realize that the heat in Florida would cause you to have an odor?*" He said, "No." He had not realized that the heat in Florida compared to Switzerland would affect his scent.

After the conversation, we looked at each other and laughed. We went right out to the store and bought deodorant and a shaver to shave some of his facial and body/underarm hair. I actually became his image consultant after this. I taught him about fashion, how to wear his hair, and how to groom himself to be more pleasing to the eye.

Mr. Swiss taught me something and I taught him something about scents, body odors, and culture. He taught me to be more considerate and relaxed in situations instead of confrontational.

It was great! We supported each other.

After hanging out for so many days, coming to my house early and him staying late until my parents kicked him out, my mom asked Mr. Swiss an important question.

Mom: "*What are your intentions for my daughter?*" *I gave her a million dollars what will you give her?*"
Mr. Swiss: "*I will work hard and give her two million.*"
Mom: "*Great answer. I'm at peace.*"

This question was important to my mom to ask my boyfriend because she asked this question before to Mr. Florida.

Mom: *"What are your intentions for my daughter?" "I gave her a million dollars what will you give her?"*
Mr. Florida: *"What? I can't afford her. You spoiled her, and I can't afford to give her anything especially a million dollars."*

At the time, I didn't understand what this question meant. But now, I know. Will you support and take care of my daughter the way, I supported and took care of her? Are you a hard worker, a supporter, and a provider?

Mr. Swiss answered the question correctly because he was willing to try his best to give me more than what my parents had given me. It was not about the money; it was about the effort someone puts into a relationship. Sometimes we have to ask ourselves the same question. Are you going into the relationship defeated or looking to build and grow?

Back to School

It was time for me to return to Atlanta, the vacation was over. It was time for me to go back to the place where I started my adult education. I was going back to the people I once knew. I was heading back to my comfort zone, to the school, that started it all.

While I organized my move, Mr. Swiss was there, hanging out, listening to every conversation with my soon-to-be roommates. He was there supporting me and cheering me on towards my new adventure. But he was sad that I would be leaving. He didn't say too much about me leaving; but, I knew he was sad.

I was ready to leave this summer romance, leave Tampa to go back to Atlanta to finish what I had started because I was driven to be successful, and knew love would not pay the bills.

I packed my car with all the things that I would need for this adventure and of course, Mr. Swiss was there helping me. The time came for me to say goodbye to my family and again he was there. He was my cheerleader, my fan, and my teammate. He said he would miss me and I told him that I would be back.

While on the six hour drive back to Atlanta, the road seemed dark and endless, tears ran down my face, and I wondered if he was the ONE. Was he practicing and playing in a relationship training program for two months, preparing for the love game that would never happen? Were we participating and practicing to go to the final match to become bench warmers. We had put in all that work and now we were not going to the final match. I was not going to get a trophy. WDF!?

The Trophy

I settled into my new apartment with my two new roommates; this was the first time that I had ever lived with strangers. Previously while I was in college, I lived with my brother. Living with roommates was a strange new adventure for me. I didn't care to live with someone other than Mr. Swiss, but this was my current reality. I thought I needed to do what I needed to do to save money and prepare for my studies in Social Work.

A couple of weeks passed by, I got a job, and everything was looking up. However, Atlanta was now a gray city to me. My apartment seemed to be gray and drab. My roommates appeared to be corny and cranky. Nothing seemed right, even my new job at a call center was depressing and dreary. I sat inside a cubicle thinking and wondering if he was the ONE.

Everything seemed less sexy that it had before. There was an emptiness inside of me. This was my reality. I wondered if I could continue to live in Atlanta without Mr. Swiss in my life. One night while laying in my bed talking to him, I realized that both of us were sad, lonely, and needed each other. We had quit the game (the relationship) that we hadn't truly played.

As we spoke to one another, we were emotional, and he told me that he was drawing a picture of my face so that he could remember me over time. I thought this was the most romantic thing ever.

A few days had passed and a few sleepless nights, and I kept on wondering about the future of this relationship because it had changed. It had become a long distance relationship. We had spent so many waking hours together in Florida that I missed my partner. It was a bit like death, something missing inside of me. I told Mr. Swiss this and he was heartbroken. He wanted to do something to help me get out of my depression. But he had no plan and I was already committed to my completing my education in Atlanta.

The next morning I woke up to a knock at the front door. My roommates were getting ready for work, and I decided to sleep in. One of my roommates, opened the door and screamed out, *"It's for you Timna!"* Nobody knew where I was. Who could this be?

Much to my surprise, there stood Mr. Swiss at my front door holding the picture he had drawn of me in his hands. He said, *"Timna, I want you back."* "What?" He said, *"I want to bring you back to Tampa."*

Is he was rescuing me? Is he was saving me from my adventure? I stood there puzzled, unsure what to do with my emotions or what to say.

Mr. Swiss: *"I couldn't sleep so, I got in my car and came to you."*
Me: "What?!"
Mr. Swiss: *"I asked your father's permission to come to Atlanta to get you."*
Me: "What?"
Mr. Swiss: *"I asked him if I could marry you soon. Your father told me that I can come win you back. He said to come get you."*
Me: "What?!"

I was speechless. I teared up and told him to join me in my room. We made love for the first time, and I cried. He is the ONE. We both knew that if we played the game, played it well, then he would get a trophy. He was my trophy and I was his trophy.

The Third Month

I packed up all my stuff and paid the rest of the rent money for the next couple of months and left. I also quit my job; I decided not to continue my education as a Social Worker. I made an impulsive decision to return to a city that I was not in love with, but I was in love with the person that was there. Tampa was not my city. I actually hated Tampa but, Mr. Swiss was my guy. So, I took a leap of faith and dropped everything for love.

After a couple of months hanging out and getting to know each other like it was a job. We had each realized that we wanted to be with each other. I went back to Tampa and started all over again. I found a job and created my environment with Mr. Swiss as a member of my team.

One night, while taking our nightly stroll around my parent's neighborhood, Mr. Swiss looked at me and dropped to one knee and asked me to marry him. I gave him the craziest look and said, *"What are you doing? We have no money, and I just left everything. I don't have a pot to piss in and you want us to get married?"* But in that same breathe I said, *"Yes!"*

Thoughts raced so quickly through my mind.

I left Atlanta to come back with this guy. So, why not get married? I have nothing to lose except what I have lost already; all I have is something to gain. I am gaining the love and commitment that I was longing for from someone. Okay, Timna, just say YES.

While all of this was going on in my mind, Mr. Swiss was standing there waiting for the answer.

Mr. Swiss: *"Do you want to marry me?"*
Me: *"YES. What the hell! What da F*ck?! Let's do it!"*

I was about to Live My Life 4 Real.

It was only the third month, the third month of knowing one another, the third month of the beginning of my new life with this person. Three months before, I had just graduated from college, I was single in my comfort zone, not looking to be with a White guy or even ready to actually get married. Three months ago, I was thinking about continuing my education. I was dating three guys. I was not thinking about living in Tampa and being married. There was no way that I was thinking about living at home with my parents and not having a real job or a true income. Yep. In three months a lot can happen.

Well, I made a big decision that night. We were getting married.

Several days later, we went to the courthouse and got married. We eloped on February 7, 1997. My parents had no idea and no one would expect that I would just elope with a man from Switzerland that I had just met. I only told a couple of my friends. I felt this was about us and no one else.

My parents had no idea that I made one of the biggest decisions in my life under their roof. I was living in their home and I didn't tell them. WDF?!

Love+Faith = Trust

Chapter 3:
The Reality Check
Faith + Action = Results

We were married and in love and no one knew about it except for a few. Wow, three months ago this story was not my story, this was not my journey, but it was now.

A month passed by; we kept the secret and continued to live apart. Mr. Swiss remained at my parents' best friends' house and I was still living with my parents. One night, my mom asked Mr. Swiss to leave for the night because it was getting late. A feeling came over me; I realized that I was tired of hiding and lying about our marriage. I told her, he was not going anywhere. He was staying at the house. She was surprised and had a startled look on her face. *"What do you mean he is staying here? You know my rules. At midnight he must leave."*

I said with a stern voice, *"He is staying!"* She then looked at me with a baffling look of disapproval and said, *"Timna, when he is your husband, then he is allowed to stay here after midnight."* We started arguing. I yelled, *"He is! We're married!"* She looked at me in shock and said, *"I don't believe you! Let me see your marriage license."* So, I went upstairs, shuffled through papers and came back down with our marriage license. I then yelled, *"I got the marriage license! Here! Now he can stay!"*

She immediately screamed out to my father, *"Your daughter is married. Come out of the bedroom and talk to her!"* In the same breath she turned to me and said, *"I still don't believe you. Go get the receipt."* So I ran upstairs again and retrieved the receipt and gave it to her. Now my father was in the kitchen and staring at the marriage license. Both of them were standing in the middle of the kitchen shocked and in disbelief that their daughter would go get married without their permission or blessing. My mother turned to me and said, *"Okay. He can stay; but no one should know! We will have a proper wedding ceremony for you."* I said, *"I'm already married. So why do I need a ceremony?"*

Both my parents said, *"Because you just need one!"* At that point, I realized that it was not about me, but about them.

Mr. Swiss had been standing in the kitchen wondering why we were yelling. He stood in amazement during the whole exchange. He had nothing to say but stood there looking at the whole thing transfixed. I knew at that moment that I would be planning a wedding with my mom and our marriage was real. The reality of me being a wife, a daughter who is about to be married, and someone who is now in a true committed relationship set in. There was no fun and games; this was my reality check just as much as it was for my parents. It was also a reality check for Mr. Swiss because now he had to tell his family and friends in Switzerland that he had gotten married without telling them. The secret was now out. However, the secret was still a secret because we were planning a wedding that we wanted people to attend. So we didn't tell anyone that we were already married. This secret was kept by just a few.

The reality was that we were married, and no one knew about it.

Time went on and the planning of the wedding was in full effect. We were planning a wedding for my parents, their friends, my friends, my family, and Mr. Swiss' family/friends from Switzerland. It was a big show, a big performance for everyone. However, it meant only a small thing to me. I didn't care about the wedding; I was already married. I didn't even care about the ugly orange color bridesmaids dress that my friend wanted the bridesmaids to wear. I didn't care about all the church people that my parents invited. Hey, I was already married. I didn't ask my best friend to participate in the wedding ceremony. I knew she didn't understand, but I just wanted her to watch it rather than be in it.

My best friend's feelings was hurt, but the wedding didn't mean anything to me. It was more important to get our family and friends together for this specific moment. We wanted them to meet one another. It was not important for me to gain approval or acknowledgment of my love for Mr. Swiss. I already did this by saying, I do, in front of the court. To me, it was a reunion rather than a celebration of our love.

During the time we were preparing for the wedding, Mr. Swiss and I were challenged about our love. We were poked and questioned by my parents' friends and church members. The question from my parents' church friends was an interrogation. I didn't care about these people and what they thought about my choice. Why were they so worried about my choice of commitment? Why did they want to place their judgment, their limited belief system in my world? Why did they worry so much about my choice of a partner? Why were they our biggest critics?

The Interrogation

One Saturday morning after church... Yes, I went to church. Let me give you a little background on this. I went to church because I respected my parents and I was living with them, so I respected their wishes. The one wish they had was for me to go to church each Saturday. Anyways, after church, my parents told us that some of their friends were having an after church gathering or luncheon and we were invited. Of course, Mr. Swiss and I said yes.

> Would you pass up free food? Not I, said the cat! #LOL

So we headed over to the house for lunch. Low and behold, there was an interrogation waiting for us. At first, we were unaware of what was happening. We were just happy to get free food.

While the food was being prepared, we were hanging out talking to everyone, and we noticed that everyone was asking us question after question about our relationship. The questions started to become very intrusive and began to feel endless. Church member after church member was asking us questions. WDF?!

Mr. Swiss had a line of questions to answer and I had a set directed to me to answer. This seemed like ridiculous behavior on their part.

> Can you imagine?
> WDF?!
> This was the worst free lunch ever!

Questions for Mr. Swiss:

- Why did you leave Switzerland?
- Who are your friends?
- What did your family say?
- Are they coming to America?
- Do they speak English?
- How will you pay your bills?
- Why are you getting married so fast?
- Where would you live?
- When will you get a job?
- How would you provide for her?
- How would you survive not knowing English that well?
- When will you get a job?
- How can you be so sure that you're in love?
- Do you need a green card?
- When are you going back to Switzerland?
- Are you sad that you left your family?

Questions for me

- How would you survive?
- When will you get a job?
- How can you be so sure that you are in love?
- Are you pregnant?
- Where is his family from?
- When will you go Switzerland?
- Is his family coming from Switzerland?
- Will they like you?
- Have you thought about your differences?
- Did you think about maybe he wants a green card?
- Are you going to still live at home?
- When are you planning on moving out?
- Where will you live?
- Are you sure you love him?

Why are these people asking us all of these questions? What are they getting out of this? I was so frustrated. I wanted to curse them out and ask a few questions of my own.

- Are you providing us with a house?
- Are you getting me a job?
- Do I look pregnant?
- Are you buying my plane ticket to Switzerland?
- Are you helping me to survive?
- Do you know what love is?
- Do you even like or know me?
- What do you think about our differences?
- What is your problem?

Well, as you guys can see, I was in a WDF?! situation.

I knew that if I asked them the above questions they would have reacted negatively, to say the least. I knew that I had to be on my best behavior. I knew that they were really asking these questions for my parents. The church members were protective of my parents, and they wanted to know what we were planning for our future regarding this relationship. We were the unknown and they were nervous.

Being placed under this type of scrutiny was, by far, the most stressful thing at the beginning of our relationship. It made me question things. On our drive home, I had a serious discussion with Mr. Swiss about the situation that we were in and our future.

The Drive Home

I was upset that they planted a seed in my mind that made me question my love, my union, and my decision to get married so quickly.

I started to question both of our intentions. Was he in this relationship for the green card? Did he love me? How will we survive without a job? Where will we live? I then interrogated him while we drove the 30 minutes back to my parents' home. He was drained; I was drained, upset and beside myself. I was a nervous wreck.

Before they planted these seeds. I was alright. I was confident in my conviction and sure about my decision. But now, I was defensive and worried! I started interrogating Mr. Swiss too about his intentions and our future.

We were married already! Why was I questioning everything?

I was confused but, Mr. Swiss assured me that he was unsure of the unknown as much as I was. So, I went with my gut; my gut told me once again, I was right! It will work out and we will be okay.

Naysayers will always be naysayers; you must go with your heart and not worry about what others think of you!

I knew in my heart that I was doing the right thing. It was our love that allowed me to see the light; but, it did not blind me. It was our continuous acts of kindness, support, interest, our knowledge of self, our conversations, and my inner intuition that made me feel good about our spontaneous decision of marriage. Plus, I had nothing to lose and I had gained a real relationship which I had never really had before. I knew that everything else could and would come (job, friends, a place to live and education).

Oh, small note: My mother also called the Swiss Consulate to ensure that Mr. Swiss was not a criminal in Switzerland. Thank God he was not! At first, I thought she was crazy doing this but, I know now she was just protecting me from this stranger.

Life is what you make it
SO
Trust your intuition

Chapter 4:
Who are those Strangers?

I was walking in a world of strangers, and I was a stranger to myself.

The Stranger Within

We were married in silence; my parents knew that we were married and a few of my good friends, but no else knew. We had a binding contract that seemed to be hidden and locked away in a safe deposit box only to be revisited when needed.

I was still living at home, still under my parents' roof, following their rules, and respecting their religious values. These values were not mine, or Mr. Swiss' values. But we abided by the rules that were placed on us. We were trapped under the roof with my parents' rules and regulations. Under these rules, came sacrifices and demands that were not me. I quieted myself and changed who I was as a person to fit into this mold of acceptance because they wanted a wedding and I wanted to be a good daughter. Mr. Swiss also wanted to be accepted and be a good son-in-law.

I was silently married and now feeling committed to a world that was not my own. I was a stranger to myself and the world around me.

My parents' religion is very strict and demanding of one's time and energy. I was made to join this religion as a child. Guess what? If you're reading this, I'm like you! If you're told to do something as a child, you just do it. So why, was I committing myself to do something that I didn't agree with as an adult? I'm an ADULT. WDF?! Why was I deciding on joining a religion that I didn't agree with? Maybe because, I was the good daughter! I was the person that didn't want to rock the boat with my parents at the time, and Mr. Swiss was following my lead and being the good son-in-law.

When I was in college, I became free to choose not to be a part of this religion. I wore my earring, dressed the way I wanted, and woke up on the weekend when I decided to. I was rebellious about being a member of a religious group with which I felt no connection. I was happy to be free of the criticism, the restriction, and judgment that was put on me through this religion. So why did I choose to be a part of the religion that I dismissed from my world while in college? Why did I do everything that was required to get married under this religion sector and why did I need Mr. Swiss to follow me?

Well... Respect.

We followed and abided by the rules of the Seventh Day Adventist religion during the months leading up to me getting married. I respected my parents, and I felt obligated to their wishes. Even though I was a stranger to myself and I became a member of their society. It was what they wanted, but not what I wanted.

Mr. Swiss and I reluctantly woke up each Sabbath morning. We chuckled and laughed about how we had a duty, a job, because we were obliged. My parents were funding our wedding, and I still lived under their roof. So we thought WDF?! Go with the flow!

Each Sabbath (Saturday) we woke up, Mr. Swiss wore the same brown, checked blazer, white collared shirt and green tie with black pants. He borrowed my father's shoes each week until he was able to afford his own. Each week he became someone he was not. He wore this uniform to church and he had worn this same suit the day we secretly got married in the courthouse. I had several dresses, all of which I only wore on the Sabbath. Each week we were dressed in attire that was not us. We were strangers to ourselves, abiding by the rules of the church and following the Seventh Day Adventist doctrine. We took Bible studies each Friday night. This was good because Mr. Swiss was able to learn English.

The Pastors

We went to pre-marriage counseling with two different pastors. I remember both pastors like it was yesterday. One was Panamanian, cultured, old, sweet, well-traveled and married for over 50 yrs. He was strong but not strong in his approach. He wanted to be informed rather than share. He was rooting for our love and union. He asked us questions that were informative. Each week for a month we met with him and his wife at their small, modest home. He made an effort to get to know us. He wanted to understand our values and what we represented. He was curiously sweet, but he didn't know our secret that we were already married. We didn't tell him because my parents felt that it was important to keep this secret so that the Pastor would be authentic and willing to give us his time. They knew he would eventually be the one to "marry" us at our wedding ceremony at the church.

The other was a younger African American pastor in his 50's, not well-traveled; he was divorced, stubborn and looking to retire. He seemed to be detached from his role as a motivating Pastor. I just remember that he appeared to be very judgmental and suspicious of our union. He asked us questions of race and being "unequally yoked." He always started the conversation with a scripture from the Bible that dispelled mistrust or a lack of equality. We met him several times at his small, trailer office in the back of the church. Each time, I left annoyed; I felt like we were in an interrogation room. I was always confused, defensive, and irritated. I wished I could fire him but, I couldn't fire him because he was not on my payroll. We were obligated to see him. He was the pastor of my parents' church and so, it was the polite thing to be counseled by him. I didn't like this man because he didn't have our best interest in mind. He thought that I was walking into a dead-end relationship because Mr. Swiss was not of the same faith and was not an American. This pastor questioned the probability of our relationship lasting. He was a non-believer in our relationship and it showed.

My parents were in charge and I was that little girl still living at home, following their rules. We went to church, did Bible studies, and educated ourselves on the religion all in the name of getting remarried. It was a show; we even got baptized into the denomination, not by choice, but by right. I was the good Christian daughter. I followed all the rules to please my parents but, I didn't please myself. I lost my voice, and I made Mr. Swiss lose his as well. He was a Catholic and was joining whatever religion I decided. He wanted to win love and acceptance from my parents. Which he eventually did.

Why did I willingly choose to be a part of that religion? Why did I decide to be baptized? Why did I choose to wake up and go to church each week? Did I choose these steps to ensure the happiness of my family? Was it such a perceived obligation rather than a choice?

When I think back, I was a stranger to myself. WDF!?

My Strange Parents

My parents were doing the best for their daughter and they were concerned parents. So, what do concerned and controlling parents have in common? They place their values on their children to ensure stability and growth.

I'm not saying this is bad; it depends on the child and the values of the family. Again, I don't think this was wrong of them; this was the knowledge that they had and the information they used to raise a morally, conservative, caring person. They had done what they needed to do for their only daughter. However, as a 23-year-old, it was time for me to be able to choose what was right and what was wrong for my life. Yes, you may be wondering: why they were considered strangers. Well, to me, they just were! They believed in something that I didn't and their thought processes was different from mine even though they raised me. So, yes! They were strangers!

By the way, I love these strangers (my parents) with all my heart despite their religious rituals.

The Other Strangers

Mr. Swiss' family members were on their way, traveling on a 10-hour flight. This flight was the first time for his whole family to come to America. It was their journey to meet my family and me, the other strangers. I wondered what they thought as they traveled on this 10-hour flight. Were they nervous, worried, excited, or even confused that their relative left Switzerland several months before and was now getting married to a foreigner? Yes, I was the foreigner; me, Timna, a foreigner. Can you believe it?

When I think about it, I think they must have been questioning my interest in their son/grandson/nephew, just as much as my family.

Today, I know that they had no expectations other than knowing that they were venturing out to someplace new. They only thought about the opportunity to explore a new land. Remember there was no cell phones or computers that were accessible like we have today. There was no way of being connected to the world the way we do so almost effortlessly in our current society.

It was time for them to arrive, I was waiting worried, biting my nails, wondering about these strangers.

What would they say about our union?
Will they accept me?
What are their personalities?
Do they look like Mr. Swiss?
How will we communicate?
What are their values?
Will I get to know another part of this man I call Mr. Swiss who is now my husband?
What will they expect of me?
Should I smile?
Should I give them a hug?
Hmmm, maybe I should learn some German words.

Oh well, we'll see!

The plane landed and we met them at the airport. It was a bit strange because they had a different style than what I had pictured. They were very simple looking, almost boring, not what I was used to. They looked like they were from the country. Believe it or not, they wore Levis jeans. This was not a problem, but I thought only small town folks wore Levis.

Now it was time for the introductions to begin. Mr. Swiss introduced me to his mother first. She had red, unnatural streaks in her hair, which was a bit funky. It really wasn't bad, just somewhat outdated. Mr. Swiss' family reminded me of farmers or people from a small town with no contemporary stores available.

Then I met his grandmother, a full figured woman in her late 60s. She seemed old because of her attire and walked slightly bent over. She was a short, little lady, but her spirit was strong; she had dyed black hair that was clearly way too dark on her gray bob. She appeared to be a hard worker, someone who worked long hours for a living. Still, she was pleasantly happy!

He then introduced me to his uncle and aunt, who were clearly smokers. I wondered if Mr. Swiss had been a smoker before he met me and had withheld this information from me. They were shorter in height and slim, with smoker fingers and teeth. I would categorize them as workers, because of their hands. My mom had told me that you could always tell what jobs people do based on the condition of their hands. Mr. Swiss' aunt was very skinny. She had an unusual yet unique haircut with one long braid on the side, while the rest of her hair was in a cute. It was Halle Berry style. It was very different. Her boyfriend accompanied her. He was tall and a bit goofy, with a funny and witty personality. He arrived with his two daughters, who were smokers as well. They looked like tall, skinny, teenage European models.

Despite the outdated clothing, they were warm and inviting. I felt the beauty inside of their souls. Their smiles showed their warmth. They had welcoming handshakes. I later learned that a handshake was a cultural norm between family members. Years later, I replaced the family tradition of a handshake with a hug. The handshake was just too cold for my taste when greeting family members.

Hey, guys! Are, you awake? Are you still reading?
Don't you love a great embrace? I do!
The touch between you and other! A great hug makes your day!

I hope you get what I'm saying. Mr. Swiss' family were simple people and very sweet.

Side Note: Oh, I forgot to tell you that, Mr. Swiss didn't look like his family. For a second, I questioned whether they were strangers.

The Strangers Meet

My parents and Mr. Swiss' family finally met in person after the church ceremony at the rehearsal dinner. Actually, before the rehearsal dinner at my parents' house, my mom had called Switzerland using a translator from her job who spoke German.

My mom, who is very spiritual, wanted to get to know the woman who mothered Mr. Swiss. She wanted to have an impression about his mom before they met in person. In this conversation, my mom asked several questions which Mr. Swiss' mom gladly answered.

The number one question asked was, *"What do you think about your son marrying a woman who was of a different ethnic background?"* Mr. Swiss' mom responded, *"You can't come between love and the cards."* My mom was pleased with her answer and her energy. She immediately knew her daughter was in good hands. However, my mom was not a fan of the tarot cards.

Mr. Swiss' mom had questions of her own, like my birthday month, day and year. She wanted to pull my cards to find out if we were a good match. Yes, she was spiritual like my mom, just in a different way. She was into the stars and tarot cards. She was someone who lived by the signs of the universe. She studied my numbers to see if they would match Mr. Swiss' numbers. They did!

We were a match!

After these conversations, both of them was thrilled to meet each other in person.

The rehearsal dinner this was an intimate dinner with my immediate family and his family that had come from Switzerland. My mother purchased special dishes for this small gathering. She made traditional Caribbean food but the vegetarian version. Baked Macaroni and cheese, a vegetarian curry dish, rice and beans, beet salad, carrot cole slaw, and her traditional tambourine juice. My mom prepared meatless meals for this particular dinner because his family was worried about the mad cow disease that was rampant in Europe at that time. I don't know if you remember, but quite a few people stopped eating meat because of mad cow disease and the price of beef increased. Plus, in Switzerland, the price for beef was extremely high. His family requested vegetarian meals because they were very cautious about contamination. Remember there was no internet and there was a lack of information shared throughout the world, especially the information about the countries not experiencing this mad cow problem. Beef was not expensive in America nor was there a problem with mad cow disease. But Mr. Swiss' family was not aware of this so they also told him that they were not eating meat so that it wouldn't be an expensive rehearsal dinner.

Mr. Swiss' family brought lots of chocolate, cheese, and other associated goodies from Switzerland and Germany. They came bearing gifts from their culture. They also brought pictures of Mr. Swiss when he was a child and pictures of his immediate and extended family. The pictures told a story and gave my family and me a glimpse into his upbringing. Remember, there was no Facebook, Twitter, Instagram, Snapchat or social media to assist with this.

The doorbell rang and my parents opened their home to these strangers who would now become our extended family. Everyone embraced like they were old friends. Even though there was a language barrier, the language of love and friendliness was expressed in great detail. Mr. Swiss was the only one who was able to translate back and forth throughout dinner. He was the sole connection to the families. He was the translator. This was his job. It was a very stressful job because he had to express thoughts and feelings across two languages.

This was strange for me because I had questions for his family. I had a concern regarding the validity of the translation whether it was without bias or judgment from Mr. Swiss. I was questioning whether he was translating what he wanted me to hear or exactly what they said. I also wondered if he was asking the right questions. I had to trust him and also trust my intuitions, body language of his family, and the energy that I experienced while communicating with them.

The funny thing is that my family and his family talked during this rehearsal dinner. They didn't speak the same language, but they laughed, giggled, and smiled. Mr. Swiss' family didn't expect much because they were just happy to come to America. It was their first time in America; for some of them, it was their first time on a plane. They were especially happy because they came to Florida where there are beaches which many of them had never experienced. Florida has a great relaxing atmosphere and cheap motels when you're on a budget. Talking about cheap Motels; Mr. Swiss' aunt's boyfriend picked the cheapest hotel to stay in and was happy with it. You know the motel that looks like the Bates Motel? Yes, that place looked crazy.

Maybe I thought it was a low-class motel because I'm somewhat bougie.

#JustSaying #RealTalk #LOL

The Wedding

Our wedding day arrived three months after the night I had stood in the kitchen confessing my union with Mr. Swiss to my parents.

Mr. Swiss' mother, grandmother, aunt, aunt's boyfriend and his kids, uncle, and soccer friends came to celebrate. I was just as happy for them all to get to know my family as I was to get to know all of them.

My friends came from all over to celebrate and to meet Mr. Swiss. The unification of two contrasting families was quite a spectacle to witness; one side Swedish, not speaking English, quiet, reserved and the other Caribbean, loud, friendly, and entertaining. What a wedding! There were 200 people and what a multicultural celebration we had. Six months before this ceremony; the guests had no idea that we had found each other or that they would be at a wedding in the United States celebrating our love and our differences. We were two unexpected strangers that met in an unexpected place and fell in love.

We partied and celebrated with friends after the wedding. We didn't have the traditional honeymoon because we had to entertain his non-English speaking family and my friends wanted to hang out and stay as well. So, like everyone who visits Florida, we went to Disney World.

We fell in love with Orlando after that initial visit with his family. We moved to Orlando just one week after the celebration. Yes, we were being spontaneous again.

Mr. Swiss friends helped us to move our two suitcases into the our new apartment. We moved into a small apartment without a job, no money and little expectations of the future. We used the money that we received from the wedding to pay for the first two months of rent and utilities. We were very grateful for the pots, pans, dishes, towels, and other home goods that we received. We spent $500 that I had in savings for a futon that we slept, ate, and chilled on. This was our life for the next couple of weeks.

Despite starting a life together without money, a job, or a future plan, things moved forward very fast. I found a job as a teacher and Mr. Swiss was hired to play on a soccer team. He also found a second job as a water softener door-to-door salesperson. We bought/found furniture at garage sales, some of which we still have today. Some people gave us stuff for free. I think it was because we were young and sweet. We even found a brand new mattress in the front of our apartment. Things started to look up.

It was time to GET NAKED, to move into a dimension of uncertainty. It was time to move into this new world with faith, the action of love, and the desire to succeed.

If your mind, your heart, and soul don't align then, it's not for you! But if they do... GO FOR IT!

Chapter 5:
Breathe

In order to breathe, you must take a deep breath

It was now time to build the team (friendships, and community) and grow the business of our relationship.

As time went on, we were living together in the sight of God, as my parents would say (officially married under the church). Two years had passed quickly. I felt that it was the right time to build our family. I was ready to have a baby, and it was my time to shine as a mother. Mr. Swiss had a stable job as a marketing sales person, I was a high school teacher, and we were making a real income. We had also just purchased our first home. It was the right time to start a family.

So, like so many young couples, we practiced every day to achieve our desired outcome which was to become pregnant. We tried and tried. At first, we had fun trying; it was fantastic. However time slipped away, and the fun became annoying. It didn't happen for us. Months passed and it was not happening! We were not successful in getting pregnant at all! My best friend, Mrs. Period, came faithfully to visit me each and every month. After six months, we became concerned. We visited a gynecologist, and she told us that since we were still young, we must continue trying without assistance for one more year. The doctor said that she couldn't do anything until we tried having unprotected sex for one year. **Shit!**

Hadn't we already been having unprotected sex for more than one year?

Well, apparently our sex life needed to be documented. So we tried and tried. We used ovulation kit after ovulation kit trying to achieve a pregnancy.

This shit became real and sex was not fun, but a job to get pregnant.

There was no intimacy in our relationship just the stress of getting pregnant. Trying to conceive a baby was our second job each month. It became a ritual to have a child. WDF?! Seriously?! Sex was no fun!

The Ritual

Yes, we had a sexual ritual. Get the ovulation kit, check it each morning, when it was time to ovulate, contact Mr. Swiss, and make sure he is ready to deliver his sperm into my tunnel. Pregnancy was by any means necessary-- the task had to be done. After the delivery of Mr. Swiss' sperm, I would then lay in a ridiculous position, legs up for 30 minutes to an hour, just in case, some precious sperm would fall out. I kept myself upright to ensure excellent collection of the deposit of his sperm. Really?! WDF?!

Yep!

This was my life. This was my second job.

The stress and determination of getting pregnant was in full effect. The year passed by: we bought our first home; we adopted two kittens; and still no pregnancy, not even a miscarriage. Nothing was happening and so we went back to the doctor to inform him of our lack of success. The doctor was confused about our situation because we were so young, and in excellent health; he thought our situation was strange for our age group. He asked, *"Why are you guys not getting pregnant?"* Hmmm... I was wondering that myself. Why aren't we pregnant? What is going on? What is happening? I couldn't understand our situation. I thought this would be easy. Dump the sperm in me and my ovaries will catch it. That's it! No one ever told me that this would be a job, a chore, or even a hot flipping mess of emotions. I'm young; he is young; maybe it's because we don't have the same gene pool? What was going on? Was it because he was white? WDF?!

My doctor told us to relax and not to worry about it. We were young, and we were stressing too much over something that required patience. He decided to perform several tests to weed out any possibilities of abnormalities in my uterus.

- Pelvic
- Uterus
- Fallopian tubes
- Ovaries
- Hormone Levels

I felt like an experimental doll being poked and prodded. They considered me having an unknown impaired fertility. WDF?! Really!? Seriously?! At 20 something years of age?!

I was so pissed off that nothing seemed obviously wrong. Why the hell am I not getting pregnant? This was ridiculous and it was not in my deck of cards. I was stressed and helpless to the situation. I felt lost. I was tired! I was tired of people's questions and comments on the subject.

When are you guys going to have a baby?
"You will make beautiful kids"
"Are you guys trying?"

I was screaming inside. DON'T ASK ME WHEN I AM HAVING A BABY!!! DO YOU WANT TO HAVE ONE FOR ME?!!!

Feeling sad and helpless was not the way to go. This was not the right message for myself or my relationship. So I pulled up my big girl panties and decided to take a new look at the situation. I told Mr. Swiss, *"If we're not going to have kids then, let's party! Let's live it up and enjoy our single life together!"*

So, we decided to relax and forget about trying to have a baby. We decided to focus on our careers and move forward in building our team of friends. This was our plan, and we were on board. We met some great people. We made friends that were married couples without kids just like us. We were free! We worked hard, trained hard (fitness), partied hard, and entertained everyone.

Reality Hits and Sometimes It F*cks You Up

It was the 4th year of our marriage. Mr. Swiss and I were enjoying life and each other. We had great friends, great colleagues, excellent jobs, but we were still missing our plus one - a little boy or girl.

Time passed and the four couples that we hung out with were starting to make plans to have children of their own. It was hard for me to stomach that everyone was breaking up the party and becoming parents.

One announcement after the other...

"Timna, I'm pregnant!"
WDF?!

I was getting annoyed that it was not me announcing my pregnancy. Even my friend whose husband had a vasectomy became pregnant. WDF?! Really?!

What is happening here? Why me? Where is my pot of gold at the end of this rainbow?

I was heartbroken. Not having a baby or even getting pregnant was neither fun nor sexy. I was a mess inside! All of the women around me were getting pregnant, but not me! My sister-in-law, my husband's best friend's wife, and even the wife of one of the groomsmen in our wedding was pregnant. There were like ten women pregnant around me, and it was driving me CRAZY! I wanted to pull my f*cking hair out! WDF?!

I tried to focus on staying calm and letting nature take its course. I needed to breathe. But, WDF?! Why me?!

Infertility is a Bitch!

We decided to go to a fertility clinic. Can you believe it, I was not even 30 and I was going to a fertility doctor? WDF?! We arrived at the doctor's office nervous and fearful of what he would tell us. We were young and scared. We walked in the doctor's office which was decorated in a plain, non-creative style with plain cream walls. I remember feeling empty and nervous in the waiting room. There were also a few other couples in the lobby, but they were all older than we were. I know that those couples were wondering why we were there. Perhaps, they thought we were donating eggs or sperm. Hey, we were a viable age group to get paid for donating eggs and sperm.

We appeared to be in the wrong place at the wrong time.

However, we knew that we were right where we needed to be. We knew that we were trying for several years with no success. I sat there wondering if something was wrong with me or with Mr. Swiss. What if something was wrong with the both of us? My stomach was weak; I was sick. I became very anxious about what the doctor might tell us. My breathing grew stronger every minute that we sat there waiting. I felt my blood pressure rising in fear of what he would tell us. I wondered what Mr. Swiss was going through. He sat in silence. I was completely beside myself. I felt like a failure, lonely and empty.

Then, the nurse called our name. Being in this the doctor's office was one of the strangest situations that I ever encountered at the time. He seemed puzzled as he asked us questions about our sex life, health, and family medical history. He didn't get it. He immediately determined that we didn't need treatment because of our age and healthy lifestyle. He felt that we were too healthy and too young to go through in vitro fertilization (IVF).

What? Excuse me! Do you know what I've been going through? WDF?!

This doctor had no idea of the pain that I was in; I wanted to have a child, and I wanted my kids while I was young. Now!

Sometimes God is not ready to give us what we want when we want it because we may not actually be ready to handle what he gives us.

Mr. Swiss and I continuously talked to the fertility doctor; we kept on coming back each month telling him how serious we were and that we needed help to move forward in the fertility process. Once again, I was put through a battery of procedures and tests. They were not fun at all! I felt like a test subject in a lab.

Pelvic
Uterus Laparoscopy
Fallopian tubes
Cervical Mucus
Ovaries
Ultrasounds
Hormone Levels
Hysteroscopy

The list goes on and on.

Dang. This is a lot of work for a test tube baby!

Months passed and still they could find nothing wrong with me. You may be wondering, if Mr. Swiss have a semen analysis. Yes, he did. That was one of the first tests that had to be run because many men have a low sperm count. The test results indicated that his sperm were "lazy." The next step was to "wash" the sperm and then the "washed" sperm would be artificially inserted inside of me. Before the insemination procedure, I took a medication called clomiphene. A drug was given to me to increase my ovulation. While taking this medication, I could almost feel my eggs growing inside of me. My stomach seemed to grow overnight. Actually, I think I was just bloated. LOL I thought pregnancy was just around the corner. I think I was so excited because I knew that it was finally my turn to get pregnant.

Yippee!!

What if we have twins or even triplets?

I went to the fertility clinic. They stuck the tube in my vagina and pumped the sperm into me. I laid there thinking and dreaming of being pregnant and feeling the baby inside of me growing.

We painted our spare bedroom a mint green because I just knew we would be bringing home a baby soon.

Mr. Swiss gave me shot after shot of the accompanying medication. He even had to meet me outside of my job to give me the shot. I felt like a drug addict getting my fix from the drug dealer in the back of my car. This was our situation. This was what we had to go through to have a baby.

Drugs, Stress, Fear and Secretiveness.

Months went by, try after try but nothing. My friend, Mrs. Period, arrived like clockwork. Just nothing. My excitement turned to sadness, then to despair, and eventually to anger.

I was angry about life, my life, my dreams, my hopes, and my fears.

I had a great job at Full Sails University, good friends, a cute house, and an amazing community of people that I met in my Master's of Science Program, but I felt alone and empty.

Mr. Swiss was worried about me and our relationship. He noticed that I had given up on us, our relationship, and the hopes of having a child. I was not a nice person in my darkness and he was concerned. He tried everything, but I was done.

The Big Move Across Country

One day, Mr. Swiss came home and said, *"Let's sell the house and move to California!"* I screamed, *"What the hell? Let's do it!"* A breath of fresh air blew across me. I knew this was meant to be, because when I was a teenager, I had told myself that one day I would live in California. Checkmate! My dream is coming true!

Then I wondered how we could move to California with no jobs and no family infrastructure. After the excitement died down, Mr. Swiss sensed what I was thinking. Then he explained that he would get a transfer from his job and we would live cheap with the proceeds from the sale of our house. We could start over. He said, *"You can find a job there and we will figure it out. Let's be one again."*

We embraced. Both of us knew that we needed a fresh start. We needed a new adventure, and we needed to put this baby thing behind us in order to move forward.

So, we put our bright yellow house up for sale by owner; we painted the interior and exterior ourselves with another customer's "oops" paint. This house was our beginning, but not our end. We knew that we would find peace in the desert of California.

We sold the house in just a month, I quit my job at the University, and said bye to my family and friends. We packed a U-Haul with our belongings and made the road trip from Florida to California with the cats on our laps. I knew everyone thought we were crazy. But I was tired of going to baby shower after baby shower, feeling sad for me, but happy for their pregnancy. I was depressed because I couldn't have a child.

Palm Desert!

We drove up on the road toward Palm Springs, and it was my first time seeing windmills, the large, white windmills turning and blowing the wind. I knew this was a sign for me to breathe, to take in the warmth of the dry heat, and not to worry about having a child. I needed to enjoy my blessings of having a good life with the freedom of being together in my relationship with myself, my cats, and my husband.

We moved into a two bedroom apartment, we didn't have much, but we had each other and our two cats. For some reason we didn't unpack much, I think we knew deep down inside that we would be moving again soon. The apartment was a cute L-shape, two bedrooms next to each other, two bathrooms, a small kitchen with a bar that flowed into the dining room/living room combo which led straight out to a balcony that overlooked the courtyard. I loved this balcony. I sat there many days thinking about our future. I also, continued to think about our unborn child. Even though the thought of having the baby consumed my mind, I was very present in our new adventure. I started working out like crazy. I had a complete fitness and health plan to get my body right and one with the universe.

This apartment represented something peaceful to me. I remember our Hispanic next door neighbor who always wore a sweet cologne. I could smell him when he walked up the stairs while I sat on the balcony. I remember him always embracing his wife and her loving the way he smelled. His scent reminded me of the love one has for another. I knew that he loved his wife and she loved him.

Since Mr. Swiss was in the restaurant advertising sales business, we met incredible restaurateurs; they were people who were older than us and didn't have kids. They were fun individuals who loved hanging out, eating great food, dancing, and singing karaoke. I enjoyed myself; we were living a dream. We had so much fun with our new friends! I felt free of the worries of having a child. We hung out at an Irish pub a few times a week, our friend's fine dining Italian restaurant, and an exclusive steak house. Yes, we were hanging out with the who's who of Palm Springs. Enjoying life, I found a job working with the adult high school teaching and counseling young people who were getting their GEDs; this was my baby. Life was looking up for us.

Then, I noticed that I was eating a lot of ice. I was craving ice and went to see my doctor, and he told me that I was anemic. I had fibroids.

WDF?! Really?!

So, I went to one of the most highly recommended gynecologist in the area to seek treatment for the fibroids. He told me that I had two choices. The first option was uterine fibroid embolization (UFE), an invasive surgery that would cut off the blood flow from the fibroids and cause them to shrink. This procedure carries a risk of damaging an ovary or even the uterus. This would make it much harder to get pregnant and also create a higher risk for pregnancy problems in the future. The second option was to have a hysterectomy.

EXCUSE ME!!

A Hysterectomy is the removal of the whole uterus. WDF?! Are you kidding me?!

I started to panic. I looked at him and screamed *"I am 29 years old and I've been trying to have a baby for the last six years! I don't think so!"* Then, I asked him, *"What is the average age of your patients?"* He said, *"Forty plus."* So, then I said, *"Okay this is where you went wrong. I'm young, and I would like to keep my uterus intact! Plus, I am going to have a baby. I will seek treatment from someone else. You will not butcher me and leave me to die inside and out. That will not happen to me!"*

I left his office in a rage!

I cried all the way home and contacted Mr. Swiss in fear and panic. Then my job started again, which was to prove to the world that this was not my fate. I was going to have a baby. I decided to seek alternative health methods of removal or shrinkage of the fibroids. I went to Los Angeles to ask for help from a renowned herbalist and his team. They recommended a treatment of herbal supplements and liquids with a diet plan for 30 days. I decided to do the treatment and I never shit so much in my life! I started to lose weight, get depressed and weak! This shit (no pun intended) was not for me! I lasted for two weeks and then I was done! My mind and body were not mine. I couldn't deal with all that shitting, not eating, and vitamins. I didn't have the faith or the willpower to continue on this path of trying to shrink the fibroids naturally.

Mr. Swiss was dying inside because I was at it again, seeking extreme alternative methods to solve my problem. Yes, I was an extremist when it pertained to these two things! Pregnancy and my health.

I then decided to research my fibroid problem a little further and to seek the help of a reproductive endocrinologist. Since I had fibroids and unexplained infertility problems, this was the right specialist for me. He dealt with both of my problem areas. I drove two hours to meet this doctor to see if he could treat me. They had to perform a series of tests to determine if he could safely perform the fibroid surgery and also resolve my infertility.

After undergoing the tests, he was unsure about my success for pregnancy. He told me that he would try to make sure that my uterus remained intact during the UFE procedure. He was hoping that I was not going to have scarring in my uterus. If I had any scarring, then I would not be able to undergo IVF. The IVF procedure is where my eggs would be removed from my uterus and then joined with sperm cells from Mr. Swiss in a test tube in a lab. The cells fuse to form a single cell called my little zygote. My little zygote will start to divide, to become my embryo. My embryo is then placed into my uterus in HOPES of attaching to start my much-desired pregnancy. This was my dream.

Everything is not for everyone!

Well, it was that time, the pre-op for my surgery. We drove to the clinic and then the doctor came in to prepare me for the surgery that would be performed on the following day. He walked into the room with a mask on his face.

Hmmm...

I asked if he was okay. He said, *"Yes, I'm just a bit under the weather. I decided to wear a mask so I don't contaminate you."* He said this with a smile and a chuckle. Nope. That was not funny!

Mr. Swiss and I looked at each other.

We said, "No, we will not have this surgery." The Dr. looked at us and asked why. I explained, *"I'm not comfortable with this situation."* Then he said, *"But you would now have to wait another month or so for me to get you in."* I said, *"That's fine with us."*

We walked out of the office and never returned. My spirit didn't feel comfortable with this situation. I knew he wasn't the one to perform this surgery. I decided to wait and look for another surgeon. I realized that my surgery was not a life or death thing so I could wait.

During this time my very good friend from college contacted me to tell me that she was pregnant and expecting sooner than later. She asked me to come to her baby shower. I was to be the Godmother for her child. Hmmm, I thought maybe this might be my role for the moment, a Godmother!

Then the day came. It's a boy! She asked me to spend some time with her and the baby after the delivery. Of course, I did. But something seriously wrong happened.

Her husband disrespected me and inappropriately approached me. He slapped me on my butt and he tried to come into the bathroom when I took a shower. All of this happened when my friend left for a brief moment. I was shocked and hurt by his disrespectful ways knowing that his wife just had a baby.

I was conflicted:

Do I tell her? Do I reveal to her that her husband was a dog? I thought nope. This too shall pass. I didn't say anything to her and left her home earlier than expected. I couldn't fake it! Her husband was a DOG!

A few weeks passed and one day she called me, crying that her aunt wanted to leave her home. Her aunt disapproved of her husband and his ways. She asked me what I thought about him. I told her, "*I don't trust him! Don't ask me why, but I don't trust him!*" She was so upset that she called him on the phone and started yelling, "*Why does Timna think that you're not to be trusted?*"

He spilled the beans but with a big assed lie. My friend called me back and told me that he had said that I had been trying to seduce him, that I opened the door to the bathroom and asked him to come in wearing just a small tee shirt. He told her I was flirting and wanted his attention. WDF?! This was ridiculous. I couldn't believe what I was hearing. He was blatantly lying about me. We started to argue and she decided to take his side. This hurt my feelings, and I knew that we couldn't be friends. We had to end our friendship, and I renounced my "Godmothership" (I made this word up). I no longer wanted to be a part of that relationship. I couldn't understand why she wanted to put up with his crap (lies).

NOW I DO! It's hard to leave when you just had a baby.

Months later, I turned 30!

I remember my 30th birthday like it was yesterday. Someone told me that when you turn 30, there is a moment in time where you look back and evaluate your life. During this period of reflection, many people start to cry and become depressed. Because their life at that point is not where they want to be.

Well, years ago, I thought this couldn't and wouldn't be me crying on my 30th birthday. However, I was in my car driving from Beaumont California to Palm Springs, I saw the windmills in front of me and the road was clear, the sun was setting, and it happened. While I was driving, my mind became flooded with thoughts of accomplishments and failures. Yes, I started to cry because I thought of myself as a failure when it pertained to having a baby. I was a failure.

What happened?
Why am I not getting pregnant?
I want to be a mom!
What is going on?

Then, the phone rang the voice on the other end was Mr. Swiss who said, *"Meet me at the Irish pub."* I wiped the tears from my face, drove over to the bar and when I walked in, there it was a big party! It was a surprise birthday party! All of the people we met in Palm Springs and Palm Desert were there. It was a night of Karaoke, drinking, and laughter.

I looked around and noticed the old couple that had been coming to this bar for years. This couple had been married for 50 years. I started to tear up as the tiramisu cake came to the dance floor. Happy 30th birthday Timna. Timna, you should be crying for joy, not sadness. You have a good life! I scolded myself because of the thoughts that caused me grief. I didn't appreciate what was in front of me and what was behind me!

As time went on, my feeling of sadness about not having a baby returned and something happened to Mr. Swiss. He was not happy. He became a stranger. I had no idea that I was ruining our relationship with my obsession. He couldn't speak to me about our problems; he just held it in and retreated to his job. He was lost.

He was lost and I had no idea because I was in my world, not even noticing his descent into darkness. He was working hard to provide for us but losing himself in the process. He was missing for hours at a time, even days. Yet, I had no idea that he was not at work. I just thought he was a workaholic. I trusted that he was there.

One night, I was sitting in our two bedroom apartment, reviewing our bank and credit card statements and double checking our finances. This was something that I did every six months to make sure that we were on track financially. But something was different this time. We were missing some money. Money had been taken out of our account that could not be accounted for. So, I called Mr. Swiss, who was traveling, asking him about our financial situation. I asked him about the large sums deducted from our checking account. I asked him why there were cash advances from our credit cards. He immediately started to cry and say that he was sorry. Sorry for what?"

I was sitting in front of my computer in anticipation of what he was going to say. Did he have a lover? Hmmm... I told myself, I can handle that because I have been sexually distant and focused on having a baby. I get it.

But it was something more painful in my world.

He told me, *"I'm gambling, and I can't stop!"*

WDF?!

I was SHOCKED.

I couldn't breathe.
My mind went blank.
Then, I became angry.
I felt my blood pressure rising.
How could he have done this to me?
How could he have lied?
What the f*ck is wrong with him?
Who does that?
Who the f*ck gambles?
That's just STUPID!
What's wrong with him?
Who does that?

I felt betrayed.
I was lied to.
I was super angry.
I wanted to scream, to cry, and to curse!
The walls closed in on me.
WDF?!

I then went directly into Fix It Timna Mode. I became Super Wife, the helper, the supporter, the forgiver, the make-it-happen, woman!

I told him, "What do you want me to do? How can I help you? Come home! Let's figure this out!"

Deep down inside I was super hurt and I felt super betrayed. I felt like I was sleeping with a stranger, the enemy, a liar, a deceiver, someone who was hiding his dark side and having an affair with the Casino. The crazy thing was that I knew I was going to accept him back because I felt like I contributed to his demise.

Before this, if someone had asked me what was one of my zero tolerances in a relationship, I would have said the loss of FINANCE, gambling. This was my number one. I had to face it. It was my zero tolerance and yet I accepted him back. I wanted a baby. I loved him. He had a sickness. I could forgive him. We could do this.

I wanted his baby.

I will never forget the pain and the stress that he caused me, constantly looking for him and checking our accounts. The stress I was under seemed almost unbearable yet, I push through it. Although I knew that our love and my trust for him would never be the same. This was a bad dream. I forgave, pushed it under the carpet, and decided that he had a sickness and needed my help. I became Super Wife and held onto this role for years to come.

Pull up your big girl panties. Life must go on.

A few months later, I forgot and forgave him. I felt like I had everything under control. The accounts were stable and, of course, I went back to focusing on having a baby. I also needed the surgery for my fibroids, but I could not find the right doctor. Then something happened. Mr. Swiss was presented with a great opportunity in Las Vegas.

Las Vegas? Sin City? Is this a good thing? Should we move? Is he going to be sneaking around with the Casino again?

I had finally gotten the gambling under control; I didn't want to mess things up. But I was thinking about the salary of course. I knew that we could replenish what he had lost with this new job. Woooohooo! Why not go to Vegas. There would be more partying, more fun, and more ways to forget about our troubles.

We both said, *"Yes!"*

Vegas Baby!

We packed our bags and were ready to go. We found a great apartment that was larger than the one in Palm Desert. It was a mini townhouse with all the makings of a typical starter home. It felt like home.

Now, it was time to press the restart button. However, we were still unhappy and drowned our sadness by hanging out, partying, smoking weed, and drinking. We were happy on the outside, but we were both sad on the inside.

I insisted that Mr. Swiss see a counselor for his gambling problem and I sought counsel for my issue. I found a reproductive endocrinologist for treatment. He told me that I was the perfect candidate for IVF. He said that the first step would be to remove my fibroids while keeping my uterus intact via uterine fibroid embolization (UFE). After this, he was sure that I would get pregnant and have a healthy baby. We both felt comfortable with his ability and faith to achieve pregnancy. We scheduled the laparoscopy to harvest the eggs after I recovered from the UFE and I called my dad to come and nurse me back to health through the six-week recovery process.

At this time, I had no idea that Mr. Swiss was completely stressed out about the whole situation and was unable to share his feelings with me. He was beside himself with fear. He was unable to communicate his reluctance about having children to me. He was not prepared to be a father. He was terrified of the thought of bringing a child into this world. At that point, we had been married for seven years; you would think that he would have said something because most of these seven years, we had been trying to have a baby. He just wanted to be free of this situation and Live Life 4 Real, with just us two.

While Mr. Swiss was silently stressing, I was recovering from my UFE surgery. It was a success! I could see the pot of gold at the end of the rainbow. One more procedure to go.

It was happening I could feel it!
I could touch it!
I knew it was happening soon!
The excitement filled my soul.

I had a party at the house to celebrate my recovery.

But, something held us up!
FINANCE
There was no romance without finance.

We were broke! We couldn't afford the IVF treatment. I was pissed! I was so mad that I got rid of our cats. I lost my mind! I went CRAZY for a second! What is going on? WDF?!

Why are we broke? I hadn't had a steady job and was relying on Mr. Swiss for financial stability, emotional stability, friendship, and everything else in between.

Mr. Swiss broke out in hives the night he told me that he was gambling again. He had continued his love affair with the Casino, hidden from me. He was hiding in the dark, staying out late, lying and sneaking behind my back to see his lover. We were broke and he knew why!

His girlfriend, the Casino, had broken my heart again.

Mr. Swiss cried when I gave the cats away. He didn't say anything after that; he shut down and went silent. He allowed me to go emotionally crazy. He had no idea what to do. All he wanted to do was make it better; but he couldn't. I was a mess, and he was too.

Once again, I forgave him and he forgave me for giving the cats away.

The New Beginning

Eight months later, a new opportunity came for him to work with a new company, a startup. He jumped on the opportunity because we needed better insurance and a better income. We needed to live in a place where there was less partying, no casinos, and more stability for the both of us. This new company asked him to move to Atlanta, and I knew this was a perfect place because it was where it could all happen. I had connections; I could get a job and we could buy a house. I knew that the best doctors would be there and we would finally be able to start a family.

Hot-Lanta

We were off to Atlanta for our new adventure.

Restart, Renew, Redo, Refresh and any words that you can think of that mean Rebirth.

We were ready for our new start; it was time to replenish what we had lost: our faith, our financial stability, our love, and our life. Now it was time to Live Life 4 Real. We rented a small apartment where we decided to start fresh. Mr. Swiss settled into his job, and I found a job that was right for me. We stayed in the apartment for two months and then we bought our second home. We moved in on the night of the biggest ice storm that Atlanta had ever seen. Yes, we were those people moving in dangerous conditions. But we had a focus, a need, and we wanted to move forward.

I started to see a new reproductive specialist who was impressed with the surgery to remove the fibroids that the doctor in Las Vegas had performed. He was ready to move forward with the IVF process. However, he asked us to do one thing that no one ever asked us to do. He requested that we go through marriage counseling. I think he knew that we had been on a rocky ride; but I was shocked.

What?! Marriage counseling?! Why? I was in denial. I believed that all was well in the our house. But deep down inside, I knew this was important for our relationship. We decide to schedule the appointment with the recommended marriage counselor who specialized in couples going through infertility.

Marriage counseling was not the end, but the beginning.

There we were at the marriage counselor's office for our first session. We walked into this building in Atlanta. The parking was a mess and we were a mess. We both felt both despair and excitement at the same time. What if, we found something out about each other that we wouldn't be able to bear? What would we learn? What would we feel? I felt a sense of fear come over me as we took the elevator up to the 10th floor. I wondered what would happen.

We walked into the office, and our therapist was an older white man who was thrilled to meet us. He was very welcoming. We sat down ready to start the session. We had looks of anxiety on our faces. But the therapist relaxed us. He told us that we were here to find out what our goals were and if they were aligned.

This might be worth it. Let me go with the flow. The therapist asked us one question that rocked my world. He asked, *"What if you don't have this baby?"* Oh, shit. What if?

We both looked at each other thinking about this question in silence. The therapist ask the question again but this time looking directly at me. I answered with sadness and fear in my eyes. Oh my goodness, I had never thought of this question or answer. What if we didn't have this baby? Then, reality hit me. It has been nine years and no results of having a child. What if we don't have this baby?

As tears filled my eyes, I said, *"Well, honestly I would try everything to have this baby and if nothing happens then I will work on our relationship and let that grow. But, God did not put me on this earth not to have a baby. So, I will have a baby!"* That was it! I was going to have this baby. I had faith!

Then he turned to Mr. Swiss, *"What if you don't have this baby?"* Mr. Swiss turned calmly to the therapist and said, *"We would adopt but I love my wife and our relationship just as it is."*

What he said made me tear up. My Swiss was thinking about me, and I was thinking about him and our future. I knew that we wanted a child but...

WHAT IF... we were unable to have a baby? Then what?

<u>Another Day Another Dollar</u>

We started fertility treatment with my cool new doctor. Dr. P was awesome. He was THE man, relaxed, confident and ready to get the job done. He advised me to seek further counseling to help me relax and release all tension for the process. He knew that if I kept this negative stressful energy, it would be hard for my body to accept the pregnancy. He was aware that we had been trying for nine years. I took his advice and decided to speak with a woman meditation counselor. When I met with her, she told me to make an appointment with an acupuncturist who specialize in infertility. They had no idea that they would become my dream team.

Dr. P was cool; the meditation counselor gave me great tools to use to relax, and the acupuncturist released the stress endorphins from my head and uterus. I also attribute my stress reduction from the conversation that we had with the marriage counselor, knowing that the worst that can happen is that Mr. Swiss and I had each other.

Now I was ready.

The big day came, it was time to have the five-day embryos implanted in me. I had only two implanted and I was excited. I prayed and laid there, nervous, my legs trembling. My doctor and his assistant were both consoling me while Mr. Swiss held my hands. I was trembling because I had doubts.

Will it happen? Will I get finally get pregnant?

My nerves took over my body and I trembled in fear.

Why fear? Because it's been nine years of drama and finally this may be it. Dr. P told me, *"Don't worry. You have ten more embryos so you can have several more tries if this doesn't work."* Not work?! WDF?!

We left Dr. P's office with instructions to follow. The very most important one was to relax. Well, I went back to work and continued my life hoping and praying that, in the next couple of weeks, the pregnancy would be positive.

Nope, it didn't happen. Mrs. Period, showed up again and I panicked. What is going on? Why are you visiting me again? Go away! WDF?!

I went back to my doctor and he told me not to worry. All the ladies in the office showered me with encouragement and support. I remember how I felt. I was sad, but because they were rooting for me, I knew that the next time it would happen. I kept believing! I decided to have full faith that this would happen. I prayed and asked God to help me to release fear and doubt, to believe that I would get pregnant and this baby would be so grateful to be in this world. I'm ready!

Then I went through another round of treatment. This time when I was in the stirrups, I was relaxed. I said, *"Let's do this! I'm ready."* I took a leave of absence from my job to release any stress that may occur and it happened! Mrs. Period decided to take a vacation! She decided to take a sabbatical!

I'M PREGNANT!
I'M PREGNANT!
I'M PREGNANT!

Joy comes in the morning!

Chapter 6:
The Arrival
When it's time, it's time

The Pregnancy!

A couple of months went by fast. I was the happiest pregnant lady that you could ever meet. I took time off from my job, and each morning I gave thanks for my unborn child. I was Living Life 4 Real: being in the present and looking forward to the future.

I was preparing for the arrival of a powerhouse. I knew this child would be powerful and bold. We painted the room a dark, brick red, which represented power. He or she would be someone who knew that their journey was a long one in the making.

It was December, and Mr. Swiss' mom came from Switzerland to enjoy my pregnancy. She was as excited as we were. She wanted to give her blessings to us by being a part of the beginning stages of the pregnancy. Mr. Swiss and his mom both wanted to ensure that I would be relaxed. I had no idea that they had another plan as well. One evening after dinner, both Mr. Swiss and his mother sat with me to discuss me not returning to work.

Excuse me?
Did you say you would like for me to be a Stay At Home Mom?
Excuse me?
This was not in my plan!

I lowered the screaming voice in my head and relaxed my face. I looked at them and said, *"I am not that woman who stays home with her child and opts out of working. My mom worked, my grandmother worked, and Caribbeans have 10 jobs! How can I explain to my family that I decided not to work?"*

They replied, that working is a state of mind. Having a child, being with that child, and raising the child the way you want to raise her or him is a job in itself. You can be a mompreneur. They didn't actually use the word mompreneur, but this was the only word that I could think of that would allow me to wrap my brain around staying at home and opting out of continuing my career endeavors.

Hmmmm....

Really?!

Let me think about this....

As usual, my brain was working a million miles a minute. I said, *"So, you are telling me that if I stay home, I would actually be working? That makes no sense! We need money. We need to maintain our lifestyle!"*

His mother then told me, via Mr. Swiss translating, that she stayed home for ten years. She was able to return to her job. In a few years, she would be retiring and she would not have changed a thing.

I thought, *"Ten years?! What will I do at home for ten years?"* WDF?!

I started to laugh to myself at the stupid shit they were telling me. I said, "Really? I don't think so!"

I took a deep breath and said, *"I will only stay home if Mr. Swiss increases his salary to the amount of money that I am currently contributing to the home. I don't want to change our current lifestyle unless I will be upgrading."*

Real talk.

Mr. Swiss took my challenge and told me that he would work harder and more efficiently. He would bring in the extra money by the time I had the baby.

We will see!

I told him that I would support him and his efforts. To my great surprise, he worked harder and longer and increased his salary until it equaled mine. So, I quit my job! This is our Naked Truth!

It's a girl

After the first trimester (yippee), I searched for the perfect OB/GYN. I was considered a high-risk pregnant woman, so I knew that I had to find the best doctor in town. She couldn't just be the best; she had to be the best and look like me. One day, I was watching the Discovery Channel, and they featured an African American OB/GYN who lived in Atlanta. Of course, she became my doctor.

I wanted only the best. It took me so long to get pregnant that I wanted a doctor who understood me on every level. Therefore, I wanted someone who could also understand me on a cultural level.

She was the one!

I wanted to feel the closest to my natural heritage as possible. I was bringing a human being into this world that needed my full love and support. I walked into the office, the doctor and her patients represented black beauty. This environment was relaxing. I was ready to continue this journey of pregnancy.

My OB/GYN cheered for me. She knew my story; the ladies in the office also knew my story. They saw the joy on my face. I was so happy to come into the office and hear the heartbeat of the baby. I was the happiest pregnant woman on earth.

This journey was starting off with a bang. The ultrasound was scheduled, and I was excited to know the gender of my unborn baby. I was completely nervous; I thought I would for sure be having a boy. Mr. Swiss was just looking forward to having a healthy baby.

I waited for the nurse to tell me that it was a boy, but it wasn't. It was a girl. Yes, a girl.

Immediately, I thought about her name. What would I name her? A name is everything! It is your soul, your power, your life!

Niami, Naomi, Ania, Ana? Hmmm… Maybe an old family name.

But first, before I got ahead of myself picking the perfect name, I wanted to start planning everything else. We planned her room, bought furniture, and bought a bigger car. We did everything we needed to prepare for the baby. I was driving myself and Mr. Swiss crazy with excitement. I couldn't sleep. I was so very excited about being pregnant.

Mr. Swiss traveled a lot and became the number one salesperson in the company. He worked effortlessly, tirelessly, to increase his salary so that we could maintain our lifestyle. I traveled with him so that he could keep an eye on me and I could keep an eye on him. Some people thought that I was helping him to get his sales because I was always traveling with him. I was his side-kick, supporting him, encouraging him, and being his cheerleader.

While my belly grew and my excitement grew even bigger, I sang, laughed, and played with my growing baby. She knew I was her cheerleader before she came into this world. I continued my meditation music every day. This helped me to relax. I also stopped watching scary movies or negative television. I just wanted my home and my pregnancy to be very positive.

We had a scare!

One night, I was home, and I had sharp pains shooting through my stomach. WDF?! Really? Are the bags packed? Isn't it too early? What is going on? I was only six months pregnant and did not want to lose the baby. We jumped into the car. Mr. Swiss was silent, but you could see the fear on his face. We were in panic mode. Of course, my doctor was on vacation which totally stressed me out. I didn't want to have this baby now! I certainly didn't want to have her without my doctor taking care of me. Mr. Swiss drove fast. We panicked in silence; the stress was crippling to us. It seemed to be the longest drive ever. We sat in the emergency room waiting to be seen; it was a nail-biting experience. We waited and waited. The doctor on duty told us that I was experiencing Braxton Hicks, which are the contractions that occur before real labor. He said that these contractions were normal in pregnancy, even in the second trimester.

What? Wait. This is Normal?
YES
Well, it was not normal for me. Excuse me!

Mr. Swiss wiped the sweat from his forehead. Our panic mode changed into relaxation. Well, almost. I had to think about it again on the drive home. This is normal? Really?

The Signs of Life

It was time for the 3D ultrasound! My belly was growing, and my anticipation grew as well. I wanted to see her. I wanted to name her officially. We schedule a 3D ultrasound. It was so posh with stadium seating. It was a full blown studio, two chairs, and a large screen to see our unborn daughter. They were ready; we were ready.

The live video started. We saw her. She was smiling inside of me! She was winking! Oh, my goodness; this was a breath of fresh air. The ladies at the studio were so impressed that they said, "*Your baby is happy. We have never seen a baby wink before!*"

Wow. I'm going to bring life into this world! Finally!

Now, I knew her name. It's IVY. I named her after my grandmother who passed away. Ivy is a vine; a strong vine. The name felt fitting: an old soul, someone who is making the journey to come into this world. Someone who waited for me and I waited for her. Finally!

It was time to plan the delivery. We were ready with our action plan. The room was ready; the first outfit was purchased. The bag was packed! We were ready!

My C-section was scheduled for a hot summer day in July. I was nervous and excited all at the same time. I remember talking a lot while we waited in the waiting room. Mr. Swiss was super quiet. He just stared at me while I nervously talked him to death.

"When I'm in the surgery, please stand by me. Hold my hands. When Ivy comes out, make sure everything is okay. Are you nervous? Why aren't you talking? Do we have everything in the bags? Do you have Ivy's outfit? Don't forget we are taking pictures. Who will we call first? Are you staying here the whole time? Did you tell them that you're going to sleep here with the baby and me? How long do you think we will be here? I hope she is healthy and everything goes well. How do I look? You need to take video. Nevermind take pictures. Wait. Take pictures of her and me when she is delivered. Are you ready?"

I talked and talked! I asked every question. Most of the questions, I knew the answer to; but I kept talking; while he stayed nervously quiet. I could imagine that all he wanted to tell me was to shut up and relax; but he didn't. He was super sweet. He just let me talk and talk and talk.

<u>The Delivery</u>

Finally, it was time to deliver Ivy.

They placed me on a rollaway bed and gave me the epidural. I couldn't feel anything, except my emotions of excitement and fear. This was the moment that I had been waiting for; it was years in the making.

As I laid there, Mr. Swiss held my hands, the blue sheet over me like a curtain waiting to reveal my star. The doctor told me to relax because she knew about my nervous chatter; she had experienced it before. She told me, step by step what she was going to do and I was definitely in the present soaking up everything as she spoke.

First, she said that she was going to wipe the area to prepare for the incision Then, she made a small incision.

I wanted to know everything.

Mr. Swiss was still silent. I started to worry that he might pass out. I kept on saying, *"Don't pass out! Prepare the camera! She needs to have her first picture taken while entering the world!"*

Mr. Swiss must have thought that I was crazy. I knew the rest of the people in the surgery room thought I was nuts. I didn't care!
The incision was made; it was time to get Ivy out.

The doctor was having trouble. She couldn't get Ivy out. I felt a slight panic in the room. The doctor called for assistance; she needed bigger forceps!

She told me, "Her head is too big! She doesn't want to come out! She keeps on slipping back in! Timna, your daughter, is fighting me; she wants to stay in!" She was saying this with a smile, but you knew she was nervous.

SPLASH...

Blood splattered against the blue sheet that prevented me from seeing the C-section procedure.

I screamed out, *"I'm dying! Mr. Swiss! Save our baby!"*

My doctor said, *"Timna, stop being so dramatic. We're going to get a bigger forcep. You will be fine! You're going to make your husband pass out. Stop it!"*

I could see the nurses. They were all smiling. It must me okay. Yet, I still felt like this was the end! I went through all of this to die. WDF?! Really?!

What is going on here?

Then Ivy came into this world screaming. They tried to clear her lungs, but they quickly realized that they didn't need to! The nurse who was clearing her lungs said, *"She doesn't need anything! This baby is making a statement! I'm here world!"* They all started to smile. I of course screamed at Mr. Swiss, *"Take the picture!!!!"*

Suddenly, there was sense of panic that came across the room. The whispers started:

Her measurement is a bit off.
Measure her again.
She won't keep her eyes close. She is so alert.
Measure her again.
What was the measurement?
Check her vitals.
She is so beautiful.
Measure her head.

Then they said, "Mrs. …. we need to take your daughter for further observation. Her measurements are off."

I screamed at Mr. Swiss, "Follow them! Don't leave our daughter!"

He then looked at me and said, "No, I want to stay with you!"

I said, "No. They said I would be fine. Just Follow Ivy!"

My doctor then said, "Timna, everything will be okay; she is in good hands."

I was on so much medication, and my emotions were all over the place.

Should I be joyful? Should I be sad? Should I be scared?

WDF?!

I passed out. I awoke in the hallway, waiting for my room to be ready. For some reason, I knew my situation wasn't typical. I quickly realized that my child had an issue. My parents were in the waiting room unaware of what was going on! If they had only known, they would have panicked too.

Then Ivy came out with Mr. Swiss. They told us that she was healthy, but they needed to run some genetic tests on her.

WHAT IS GOING ON?!

Ivy looked normal; she was super alert, she was looking everywhere, she was hungry, and she had a voice to wake the dead! So what was her disability?

Mr. Swiss was just quiet. Stressed but quiet. In silence, he tried to make sense of everything. In our room, we were waiting patiently. I looked down at my baby and started to cry, *"Why me?! Why me?! What have I done to deserve this?"* WDF?! Really?!

Mr. Swiss didn't say a thing; he just sat there with his computer and started to play games. He was lost in another world while I was crying and sobbing.

We each needed our moment to mourn what we thought was perfection.

Then, the room filled with people. Nurses and doctors crowded in. My doctor approached me with tears in her eyes. She just kept on saying, *"Sorry, I didn't know. Sorry."*

In my doctor's eyes, I knew that she knew that this happy pregnant woman was no longer happy, but crying and wanting to know what was wrong with the baby she waited ten years to meet.

Then the Geneticist spoke, and she said, *"Your daughter has Achondroplasia, Dwarfism."*

Me: *What is that?*

Geneticist: *She will be short.*

Me: *How short?*

Geneticist: *Short, Like "Little People" short.*

Me: *Okay, I can handle that but....*

Geneticist: *Well, she won't be wearing GAP clothes.*

Me: *Excuse Me! She will be wearing this dress that I bought her for her first pictures. She will be wearing GAP clothes even if I have to fix them myself. I will never deny her fashion. (smiling) But seriously, how is her brain? Does she have any mental disabilities?*

Geneticists: *No, just height restrictions. However, we will conduct more test has she gets older to weed out any other complications.*

While we were talking Mr. Swiss was researching this disability called Dwarfism! He then asked, "*So, will she have medical issues?*"

"*Well,*" the geneticist said, "*We will determine this as we go. There are so many types of Dwarfism, but the Dwarfism that Ivy has is one of the most common ones. She is healthy and beautiful. She was meant to be with you. She picked you as her parents so cherish this.*"

Mr. Swiss and I looked at little Ivy and started to cry! I think the whole room was crying because Ivy was so alert and so ready to be here!

They left the room and the photographer came in and wanted to take pictures; she had no idea what was going on. She was just making her rounds around on my floor.

She said, "*Would you like to take pictures of your newborn?*" I said, "*No. She is not ready, my husband needs to return our daughter's first dress for a smaller size.*"

She then said, "*Is she a preemie?*" I said, "*No, she has something called Dwarfism.*" She then said, "*She beautiful and she is very alert. She was here before.*" The photographer stated that she has worked for the hospital for a long time and has never seen a newborn who as alert as Ivy.

This made me think about Ivy when she was in my belly. During the 3D ultrasound, they told me that she was here before because of her winking inside of me? Yup! I realized that I had a job to do! I needed to pull my big girl panties up and say f*ck it! Let's Live Life 4 Real. Let's do the damn thang! Let's make sure this little girl, Little Ivy, will be a Rock Star! This was my job to make this happen. I was a mompreneur now for sure.

Say Cheese!

Mr. Swiss returned with a new preemie dress for Little Miss Ivy. I was determined that she would look her best for her first picture day. The photographer came back and we place a silky, soft, pink blanket on the bed, and I laid Little Ms. Ivy down. She was ready for her photoshoot. Yup. She had her eyes wide open. I knew then that this Little Girl was truly a blessing.

My parents believed that Ivy didn't have Dwarfism. They thought that the doctors were wrong that God doesn't make mistakes. I challenged them that she did have Dwarfism and that God had not made a mistake. We took a long time to have this baby and she was ours. She was ours to love, to keep, and to cherish despite her abilities or disabilities.

We had planned to leave the hospital a week after Ivy's birth. However, Little Miss Ivy was jaundiced and they wanted her to stay in the hospital a little while longer. Mr. Swiss and I refused to leave Ivy alone in the hospital. We knew that if we left, we would feel like we were abandoning her. The hospital gave us a room that was not luxurious like the original room, but we didn't care; we just wanted to be close to Ivy. The room had no bed, but it had a recliner that you could folded out and used as a bed. I was pumping my milk because they didn't allow me to nurse Ivy. The room was super quiet. Mr. Swiss and I were sitting there patiently waiting to visit Little Miss Ivy when I started to cry, *"Why me? Why me? I can't understand what is going on? Why me?"* My emotions took control of me, and I said once again, *"Why me?"*

Then we heard whispers from the adjacent room. I clearly heard the people next door.

The husband said to the wife, *"I know he can't hear or see, but he is ours."*

What? Oh my goodness, and I was crying over what? I looked at Mr. Swiss, and we both silently said sorry for thinking pitiful thoughts about our situation. We immediately became grateful for our daughter, the life we brought into this world. She was ours. Her disability was nothing compared to the child of the people next door.

You may be wondering if we met the people next door. No. The universe knew it wasn't necessary; it was only the message that we needed. God sent us a gift, and it was Ivy. She found us and she knew we would be the best parents for her. It was our job to do the best that we could do. There were NO EXCUSES.

Coming Home

We were finally back home; it was the beginning of our new adventure as a family of three. We were ready to explore this world as parents. Ivy was super little; she couldn't fit in a standard crib because it looked like it was swallowing her up. So we went out and bought her a bassinet. We were unsure of her condition, so we placed her bassinet in our room to hear her breathe. Because this was so new to us, we wanted to make sure that if we saw or heard anything, we would be ready to react to her behavior.

I nursed her and was happy to have made the decision to stay at home. I knew that decision was the right one because, I could never leave this baby with anyone. She was so tiny; but she was not fragile. She had a firm grip and a strong personality. She woke up every 2 hours for a feeding. She was a hungry baby. If you didn't feed her she would yell and scream. Oh boy, this was scary.

I remembered Mr. Swiss freaking out one day when I left him and Ivy in the car to run into the grocery store for about 15 minutes. When I returned, he had convinced himself that something was really wrong with our baby. He told me that she was screaming at the top of her lungs. He felt that something was seriously wrong. He stated that she had not stopped crying until I returned to the car. So I held her in my arms, and she started to smile. He was so pissed off. He realized that she cried like that because she wanted her mom. WDF?! He had begun to cry himself. He was having a panic attack because he thought something was seriously wrong with Ivy. He was done! This was not the first time Little Miss Ivy did this to him and others. I told people that she had healthy lungs and a strong will. She would scream to get what she wanted even if it meant freaking someone else out. This was Ivy.

As the months passed by, it was blissful to have a baby but nerve wrecking not knowing everything about her medical condition. We went back and forth to the doctor because we were unsure of so many things. The first few months of her life she had several doctor visits. We saw a neurologist, an orthopedic physician, a geneticist; she even participated in a sleep study. She also had monthly visits to her pediatrician. It was intense, to say the least.

Even though we had a baby with a lot of energy, we didn't let her and her disability hold our family back from doing everything. We enjoyed life with our bundle of joy. We went to dinners, the movies (she was super quiet), date nights, and exercised with her. The doctors said they didn't recommend for her to be in a jogging stroller but I disobeyed that and just placed two neck holders around her neck for support. I needed to exercise, and I wanted her to see the world. She loved touring the neighborhood, and people loved seeing her little body in the stroller. I remembered people asking me if she was a doll because she looked like a 'Cabbage Patch Doll' in the stroller. She also looked like a doll inside the 'Bjorn.' She was just an amazing site to see. Oh, of course, she was dressed FABULOUSLY at all times. She was my personal baby doll.

Everything was going well other than a lack of sleep. A feeding every two hours can wear on your body and your relationship.

No sex over here.

This was not my choice, but it was the situation. Plus, leaking boobs were no fun.

One night, it was Mr. Swiss' turn to feed Ivy and he was exhausted. His eyes were glossy and his body was clearly in a state of exhaustion, but it was his turn. He should not have gone out the night before (smile). The room was dark; the baby was in the bassinet next to our bed. He picked her up and started to feed her. My eyes were close next to him in the bed. I had no idea what I was going on. I heard the baby crying. I opened my eyes and I saw Mr. Swiss feeding Little Ms. Ivy feet first. Yes, this tired dad was trying to feed her little feet. He was sleeping, and he thought that he was feeding Little Miss. Ivy. I immediately took the baby and woke him up. I was laughing saying you were feeding Ivy's feet. He was startled, nervous, and shouted, *"I'm sorry. Is she okay? I'm sorry. I'm so exhausted!"* Both of us looked at each other and knew the other was thinking the same thing. Why did we decide to have a baby? Exhaustion leads you to think silly things. However, even though we both had that thought, we knew that this baby was the best thing that ever happened to us.

<u>The Scare</u>

My friend came in town, and I wanted to have a mommy break and go out with my friend. So, I asked Mr. Swiss to watch Little Miss Ivy while I had a break, a night out to myself. My friend and I dressed and I fed Little Miss Ivy. I was excited to hangout. Then....

There was a look of fear and panic on Mr. Swiss' face. He shouted, *"You can't go!"* I looked at him with disbelief and asked, *"Why not? I'm ready to leave, and you are forbidding me?"* He said, *"If you want to leave, then you will need to take this baby with you."* I said, *"Excuse me?"*

My friend looked at me with surprise as Mr. Swiss and I continued this shouting match of who was going to handle Little Miss Ivy. I looked at him with anger and frustration. I shouted, *"Fine! I'm going to take the baby. Bye!"* I walked out with Little Miss Ivy in her car seat carrier and left! We left and Mr. Swiss was astonished that I actually left. I walked out of that door with the baby; I was not letting him steal my joy of hanging out with a girlfriend.

We went to the Atlantic Station. I felt like a person again. I had taken my time getting dressed up for the first time in a long time. I had my heels on; my outfit was cute, and my lipstick was on and popping. I was ready. I didn't care about the situation; I figured this would be Ivy's first upscale outing and why shouldn't it be with her mom.

My friend and I laughed as we sipped on our Cosmos as Little Miss Ivy chilled in her car seat. I was happy that I was out of the house with a friend. I was not going to let this night be ruined.

She was the best baby anyone could ever have. Mr. Swiss was super wrong for sending her out like that. This was something that my friend and I never forgot. It also taught me a lesson.

Sometimes you have to make lemonade with lemons even if there is no sweetener.

The Surprise Move

Little Miss Ivy was six months old, and our little family was moving in the right direction. We had been living in Atlanta for 18 months and all was well. Then one night after work, Mr. Swiss told me in excitement that he was offered an excellent opportunity to move to Germany.

Wow! Germany! I thought that about how exciting that adventure would be, an image flashed before my eyes of my high school vision board. I had written that I wanted to live on the continent of Europe for five years. This was my dream and it was finally coming true. So we took the opportunity and moved to Germany. It was a dream come true. So I said, *"Let's do it!"*

It was time for us to LIVE LIFE and GET NAKED in Germany! What did this mean to me? I was unsure at the time. However, I knew that it would be an adventure of awakening, new lessons, and rejuvenation. We had a crazy past 10 years because of my heavy focus on having a child and Mr. Swiss' gambling addiction.

Now what?
What will be our new adventure?
What will bring us closer?

We rented out our house and packed up our things.

What was the worst that could happen?

What was the best that could happen?

We can do this!
WDF?!
Let's get naked!

Chapter 7:
The Longest Year of My Life

What you think this is your beginning may turn out to be the beginning of your ending.

Month One

We were up in the air the first of many 10 hour flights from Europe to the United States. The house was packed, the moving truck loaded, and our crate was on the ship. We were in the air while our material stuff was traveling by water. I felt like a voyager going to a new land with the baby in tote. It was an amazing experience. I felt free to do what I wanted to do in a new country. But was I free?

I was extremely excited. Everything was new. We moved directly into corporate housing in Frankfurt. It took six weeks for our furniture to arrive. We were in a small one bedroom apartment in temporary housing. The city was full of life. I wanted to be a part of it and what it had to offer. We were in a new city ready for a new adventure.

Being in the small apartment allowed Mr. Swiss, Ivy, and I to grow closer. During this month of closeness, we had all of the things we needed; we even had the delivery company bring Ivy's favorite toys in a special box. This was the time for our little family to get to know one another in this small environment. Mr. Swiss and I fell in love again. We communicated every day about life. We seemed to talk about everything. This small environment caused us to become closer in every way. Everything was small even Mr. Swiss' new small single room office in the city. This office was a small room that held only two desks. Little Miss Ivy would crawl and play in the room while Mr. Swiss worked. Well, I was working as well; on all the bills, unresolved issues in the US, and miscellaneous stuff on my computer. This was a great way for us to be together.

Mr. Swiss knew he had a lot of work ahead of him. He had taken on the massive role of starting a business internationally. Oh boy! What a stressful mess! Little Miss Ivy and I came to the office frequently to help with his loneliness. We gave him companionship because he spent long days and long nights getting the business up and running. We had a playpen, toys, and a sleeping mat for Ivy to take naps at the office. We were a happy little family. I was in bliss. The weather was beautiful, and the people were friendly. I was having a blast experiencing something new.

One month passed, and it was time to move into our rented townhouse in the suburbs of Frankfurt. The day the moving trucks arrived, the sun was shining, the weather was great, and it felt like a dream. We opened the door to our new home and walked around with the landlord. As she pointed out every little aspect of the house, I thought it was awesome. She seemed to care about the home that she was renting to us.

The white walls and gray flooring gave the room both a feeling of balance and imbalance. The imbalance made me feel uncomfortable. Yet, there was so much to love about the townhouse. It was four levels, a basement with a one-car garage, storage unit, laundry room, and a guest bedroom. We entered the house on the second floor, which had a half bath and a small kitchen. The kitchen gave me pause. I felt like it belonged in a studio apartment. I panicked when I couldn't immediately find the refrigerator. When I asked the landlady, she showed me a little-camouflaged door within the kitchen cabinets walls.

I said, *"Okay."* Welcome to Europe! I had no idea what a small refrigerator would mean to me and our little family's lifestyle.

On the main floor, there was the living room-dining room combo that flowed out into the backyard. Large windows were supposed to bring in natural light and had shutters that rolled down to shut the windows off completely from the outside world. The backyard was attached to four other backyards. At the time, I didn't know what these four yards would mean to my family and me. All I knew was that I was excited about being in a new country.

The stairs leading up to the third floor scared me. The spiral staircase steps were far enough apart for a child to fall through. Welcome to Europe!

Three bedrooms and a full bath took up the third floor. These bedrooms would later represent the growth of our relationship. Another flight of stairs led to the master bedroom suite, which had a balcony that led out to a rooftop seating area. When I was on the roof seating area, I could see the old 12th century fortress on the horizon. This was truly a breathtaking view. While I believed this was the best part of the house, it would later represent the silent, beautiful cage that I was in: looking at the past and seeing into the future.

This was our home; this was our new beginning and our daughter would have the luxury of being raised in a different culture. She would also be near her family in Switzerland. I knew this was our home because we were greeted by our neighbors across the street with a fresh loaf of bread, salt, butter, and a big smile, which is a German tradition when new people move in. My new neighbors said, *"Welcome to Konigstein and welcome to the neighborhood."* They spoke perfect English, and I felt welcomed.

However, while I was excited to move in, the little voice in the back of my head whispered (rather loudly): Danger ahead. Beware! Approach at your own risk! We're not in Kansas anymore! Everything was up to us to make it happen. It was our story to write. All I could think was caution; enter at your own risk but have faith that everything will be great. Again, I had a sense of balance and imbalance in this new place.

Month 2: Cash Please

The biggest eye-opening experience in moving was being lost in translation when it pertained to moving electronics from the US to Germany. We didn't realize that the electronics had different voltage levels. Instead of selling our electronics in the US and purchasing new electronics in Germany, we had to store and repurchase everything new! WDF?!

With our credit card ready, we went to the electronics store. It felt like we were buying the whole store: two TVs, two DVD players, two clocks, a stereo system, a couple of new phones, a computer, microwave, a toaster oven, and a coffee maker. We decided to max out our credit card by spending about $5,000. We thought that we would worry about paying it later. Little did we know, Germany doesn't work like America? When went to the cashier, she said (in German), *"Geld oder EC-Karte bitte."* *(Cash or debit card please.*

Excuse me! WDF?!

Mr. Swiss said, *"Wir haben eine Kreditkarte. Haben Sie American Express nehmen, MasterCard, Visum, or Entdecken?"* *(We have a credit card. Do you take American Express, MasterCard, Visa, or Discover?)* She looked at him like he had asked the most ridiculous question ever! The other people looked at us like we had two heads. They started to get upset with us. Then she called the manager and the manager said, *"Kein Geld kein Kauf!"* *(No cash! No purchase!)*

Unfortunately, all the electronic stores had the same policy. No cash! No purchase!

Sadly we had to put everything back and figure out a plan. What was the most important item that we needed? How much could we afford? What was our plan?

WDF?! Really?!

So, while Mr. Swiss went to work, I had to figure out my life at home-- something that I was new at because I had worked since I was 15. This new role called housewife was something that I needed to learn and perfect. I didn't know the language and I had no friends. I had limited access to the USA because, at that time, every call cost money and no television, no radio, no nothing. I was a free bird in a Golden Cage.

I needed patience and patience was the number one word that I lived by. With every paycheck, he helped me to bring myself out of this Golden Cage. Mr. Swiss purchased one electronic item after the other, and I figured out the system until we replenished our environment.

However, the reality was that working from paycheck to paycheck caused a strain on our relationship. We started to become stressed about not having an abundance of cash in the bank. We had to count every penny. Even though we were living the high life, we were strapped for cash. The Euro and the Dollar was all we thought about. How are we going to pay for this without stopping our lifestyle? We thought about why we left the US. We had an abundance in Atlanta, and we hadn't fought about our cash flow in a very long time.

This was a true mess!

The Inexperienced Expat

We had moved to a new country not fully understanding what would have been the best contract for an Expat (someone who works abroad). We were one of the first families to travel abroad and work for this US based company. They weren't versed on the legality, salary, and the stress that being an Expat placed on the worker and his/her family. Mr. Swiss was underpaid at the time. The inexperience of the company in an international market combined with us not knowing the financial repercussions for our household made it tough for us. Mr. Swiss was unaware that 49% in taxes would come out of his pay check. We were also unaware of the 19% sales tax on most everything you buy. Also, the exchange rate from Dollars to Euros was 1 Euro equaled $1.50. We had to transfer money from the US to Europe each month; this was a big pain in the neck. We were losing in so many directions. We felt punished for the company's inexperience in sending employees overseas. Mr. Swiss did not negotiate properly for this transition and the new role because of his lack of experience. He was afraid to rock the boat as this was a significant opportunity for both himself and his family.

We didn't fully understand what we had said yes to!

It was 2007, the year before the big market crash. Wow, we were living abroad during the BIG CRASH!!!!!! Can you believe what we were going through?

New Country
No Language
Money Issues
Building an International Company
Child with a Disability
Stay-at-Home Mom
Home in the US under water
Taxes 49% of income
High Cost of Living
No Friends or Family with the same common language
The time zone issues regarding business teleconferences

2007 was the year of blaming one another.

- Why did we rent out the house in the US?
- Why didn't we request that the company assist us in the sale of the house?
- Why didn't we negotiate better as Expats?
- Why didn't you help me see that this move would be challenging?
- Why weren't't you communicating more effectively with the Property Manager in the US?

The challenges of the tenant defaulting in the house in the US made it tough to sustain our lifestyle in Germany. Mr. Swiss' silence to the company regarding being overwhelmed made it even harder for us to breathe. Due to our struggles, this year seemed to drag on for a very long time.

<u>**My Real Reality**</u>

Our smiles were getting bleak because the bills were piling up! I opened the mail, and it was like reading a foreign language. Oh, wait, I was trying to read a foreign language. I had no idea how to decipher the bills. I couldn't pay them because the system was entirely different from America. I didn't know how to use their complicated online banking system to pay the bills. There was a code for every transaction which I had to mark off every time I use it because it was required that you not repeat the code. It was time-consuming and driving me crazy; plus we didn't have enough money to pay our bills. I felt stuck. Actually, I was financially trapped.

I was tired of calling the Relocation Specialist to help with my unanswered questions regarding basic living situations; so I relied on Mr. Swiss for my basic needs. It was strange asking someone for help on basic things. It humbled me, but it also weakened me. I felt helpless!
When Mr. Swiss came home, I would badger him with thousands of questions:

- How do I pay the bills?
- Where do I go to purchase...?
- Who do I speak with regarding...?
- Which doctor should we see?
- Which doctors speak English?
- What about daycare?
- What about the grocery store?
- What about my car?
- How do we register my car?
- What about my Driver's License?

I was stressing him and myself about these basic things.

Mr. Swiss' Real Reality

The stress was weighing heavy on Mr. Swiss. He tried to juggle work, home, and the problems in the US. He was bleak, in despair, and under water. He was so used to me being independent. In our relationship I was the person in charge of the house, finance, and any business communication. Before moving to Germany I helped him with his business emails because sometimes he needed help with his grammar. For the past ten years, we had a partnership. However, in Germany, this partnership became two solo roles.

Mr. Swiss and I had to figure out how to rent or sell the house in the US. He had to look over and translate all the paperwork in German for both his business and our home. He had to figure out the distribution of income, my daily life, and Ivy's healthcare because I didn't speak German.

The administrative strain on things that needed to get done was incredibly crazy for Mr. Swiss because he had to translate and return documents in a fast pace environment which was not his expertise. It was a one-person show in all aspects of his life. He had to build a team of great professionals from scratch. Plus he had to relearn written German. He had to translate every document from his US-based company into German plus build the pipeline of new deals. It was a hot mess, but he got it done.

Mr. Swiss was also known as Mr. Pride

Mr. Swiss had a hard time asking for things that he needed to make his life a bit easier. He felt that he could do it all. But in reality, he couldn't.
Mr. Swiss broke down one day and confided with his boss in London, but his boss ignored his pain. Mr. Swiss was at fault because he never revisited his problem or the situation after his boss ignored it. He stopped asking for help. Truthfully, he never created a full picture of his work and home life struggle for me because he was private about his pain and stress. This drove me insane! Because he knew that he had to give up the relationship to make the business successful. However, I thought he could do both if he would only ask for help.

I asked him time and time again if the company knew about our struggles and financial pain. Mr. Swiss didn't entirely agree with my tactics of asking for assistance from the company. He made excuses for them. His pride was his reality and not mine. I felt unheard and betrayed because he let his family be sacrificed for the company.

The bills at the house continued to pile up and Mr. Swiss ignored them. He became more and more stressed with building the business. I wanted to help him, but I was helpless because of the language difference. I was heartbroken because I saw him slipping away and going into his cocoon. He would be in his office in Frankfurt long hours, and he even stayed overnight sleeping by his desk. We started to argue for the first time. We even began to ignore each other. It was STRESSFUL! Mr. Swiss began to find more and more excuses to stay out late to avoid any personal conversation. His travels also increased throughout Germany. Then he started to go outside of Germany. He went to London and Paris. Then he was gone throughout the week and I just had to figure it out.

So time passed. I ignore him and he ignored me.

We seemed to have an unspoken agreement that he would worry about himself and the building of the business; I would worry about the doctor visits with Little Miss Ivy, playdates, finding friends, and the house. This unspoken agreement allowed us to find 'sun' in all of the 'clouds' that were hovering over us. We ignored each other and made it work.

My Little Bundle of Joy

Little Miss Ivy was my blessing. She was doing well. Her disability was not holding her or me back from letting her excel. As a stay-at-home-mom, I dedicated my time to Miss Ivy. I spent time massaging, developing her mind, encouraging her, and assisting her in strengthening her muscles. I told her she was a star! I don't know if you remember that *Saturday Night Live* 1999 movie *Superstar*? Anyways, for whatever reason, I thought about this movie every time I was massaging Little Miss Ivy. I would raise Ivy's little arms and scream out, "*Superstar!*" every morning and every night. Ivy would start hysterically laughing when I raised her arms and said "*Superstar!*"

In the movie, *Superstar*, the awkward, Catholic high school student, Mary Katherine Gallagher, played by Molly Shannon, dreams of dating this popular guy in school and becoming a star. The most memorable thing in the movie was when she used her fingers to smell her armpits, and then she would raise one arm up in the air, and she placed the other arm at her waist; she would get into runners split pose and scream with her hands held high "*Superstar Star.*" Mary Katherine didn't care about being awkward and strange. She had a goal to be a Superstar, and that's what she aimed for without doubt or fear.

I think deep down inside I wanted Little Miss Ivy to be a Superstar. I wanted her to be proud of who she is and to overcome obstacles. I wanted her to grow up without significant doubt or fear regarding her passions or goals. Well, I think it worked. Because her first word was, star.

My focus was on my little girl, her health, and her happiness in spite my overall dissatisfaction. I was happy just being a mom to this little girl and I didn't see how I added to the destruction of my relationship. I also only saw a glimpse of the pressure that living in Germany had on Mr. Swiss.

No German, No English

I was the foreigner in a foreign country.

One day I decided to practice my German, so I went to the local bakery to ask for simple items and have a basic conversation in German. Well, that didn't go so well.

"Hallo. Guten Morgen. Ich möchte etwas Brot zu kaufen? Haben Sie Weizenbrot haben. Wie viel kostet es?" (Hello. Good Morning. I would like to buy some bread. Do you have wheat bread? How much does it cost?)

That didn't go well at all.

My accent was preventing me from sounding crisp; you could tell that I was searching for the words and trying to pronounce them out loud in a somewhat German accent. LOL

Anyways, the Baker looked at me and said in English, *"The Bakers in Koingstein all speak English!"*

Oops! Okay then.

I told her that I was practicing my German, and if I can't practice speaking, then I can't practice my German. She then gave me the bread and continued to speak to me in English ignoring my request to help me with my German. It was a mess. I was like forget it, I took my bread and left.

No one wants to speak German to me. What do, I do?

Well, I decided to watch German TV and I learned the language as best as possible without speaking it.

I had one good German neighbor who many thought she was spacey, but she was just overwhelmed with her kids. She spoke to me in German all of the time, and this was cool. I rarely spoke back to her in German, and this was all right with the both of us. I learned a lot of words, and I started to feel more and more comfortable listening to conversations. Soon, I was moving forward in speaking and understanding German.

However, listening and not talking was one of the biggest challenges that I had to overcome. I'm a talkative person and was forced to become silent when everyone was speaking German around me. This was the most difficult thing for me to control.

I remembered having Little Miss Ivy's first birthday party, and Mr. Swiss' family arrived, and I couldn't talk to them. It was the most awkward thing ever. I had to smile and speak with my hands. At the time I had some understanding of the language, but it was difficult understanding them within a large group setting. Imagine everyone speaking to you and you're unable to speak back to them. You can only communicate while referring to a dictionary or your spouse. Mr. Swiss was the translator. He had no mental downtime because he had to manage every single conversation. Imagine long in-depth conversations happening, and you can't give any input. Plus, imagine Mr. Swiss translating and speaking continuously twice. Imagine everyone laughing at a joke, and you're sitting there trying to figure out why everyone was laughing. Plus, it was difficult for Mr. Swiss to translate jokes because sometimes it didn't have the same meaning in English. This was frustrating for both of us. I kept a smile on my face, and he kept translating. There was a lot of smiling on my part and theirs when Mr. Swiss took a break from translating.

It was a Celebration

Ivy's first birthday was awesome. It was a real celebration despite the language issues. I sent out the invitations for everyone to come and enjoy the festivities. Mr. Swiss' family was now very close to us; so it was easy for them to take a three-hour train ride or drive to our house. My parents came from the United States; this was the only time that both families came together in years.

We laughed; we smiled.

Despite our financial troubles in the first year, we traveled to France, Greece, Switzerland, Austria, and the UK and around different cities in Germany. We made it work because we were in Europe and who knew when we would be sent back to the US. Let's do it!

Ivy was talking within a year and walking by 14 months. She was doing the damn thang. Whoop whoop! Seeing my daughter grow was my day-to-day high! She was not growing that much in height but she grew a lot within her spirit.

I was her cheerleader, and she was my only friend.

The Weather

Well, months passed by and I was a bit lonely. The weather started to get cold and rainy. It became short days and long nights. Time slipped away, and the cold breeze was coming. I stayed in the house locked up because my car wasn't registered and I couldn't pass the driver license test. I became a little depressed, and started to become a hermit.

One day, my neighbor from the red house across the street rang my doorbell. He said, *"Timna! Get out of the house! Go to the mall, get some warm clothes, and buy a pair of rain boots! You can't stay in the house waiting for the weather to get better because it will take several months for this happened. So, get the right clothes, and you will be free from this house. I will also have my wife give you a sheep blanket for the baby so you can walk and travel around and don't worry the baby will stay warm."*

This was the biggest, gift anyone could ever give me. The warmth, love and advice to move forward and not hold myself back because of my perceived obstacles.

So, I did, I went to the mall and went shopping, and it felt great! I brought all of the right clothes, and I released my fear of public transportation with my baby. I purchased a more rugged stroller, and I got out of my Golden Cage.

However, something was still missing. I wanted another baby.

Another Baby

I had the right clothes, I found doctors for Ivy, and I was somewhat managing the bills. I had play dates for Ivy, but I was still missing something. I wanted another baby. I remembered Mr. Swiss and I having a conversation when we first met about wanting two children, which would be two years apart, like the way we both grew up. Both of our siblings were close in age; so, we wanted this as well. I thought about this and knew it was time, and now this became my next mission.

Two kids, two years apart.

This was my mission, but I didn't truly involve Mr. Swiss. I told him what my desires were. However, he stood silent. He was like whatever. I knew deep down inside that he was not fully in agreement with my decision. I knew he wasn't ready to add to our little family. He felt like our finances couldn't sustain another child. He became stressed about the whole idea. Yes, I knew, he was under pressure, but I was on a mission to have a sister or brother for Ivy. I figured he was not the caregiver of Ivy, so it doesn't matter. I convinced myself that I was the one taking care of Ivy. What's one more?

I went against Mr. Swiss' unspoken wishes. I decided to go ahead and investigate having a second child. I called the fertility clinic in Atlanta to see if I could come back and undergo another IVF treatment for a second child. They informed me that this was possible. But of course this cost money,

money that we didn't have. I had a will, and I knew that the means would come. I used my personal savings and credit card to pay for the second child. It was 2007; the cost was around 5K dollars, including the medication, and the insertion of my frozen eggs in my uterus. So, I went through the necessary paperwork. I, of course, informed Mr. Swiss and had him sign his life away. He was busy working, so he didn't have time to argue over my decision. He had bigger fish to fry. He pacified me so he could continue working.

So the paperwork went through, they cashed the check, my flight, and Little Miss Ivy's flight were booked; it was my time to get pregnant again.

Back to the US

We packed all of our stuff; I arranged services for Mr. Swiss to ensure his comfort in the house. I hired a housekeeper, scheduled other household services such as the lawn care, and someone to shovel the snow while I was gone. I knew he was super busy and wouldn't have time to take care of himself and the house.

I planned to stay in America from late October to the first of the year. I wanted to make sure that I was in the 12th week of pregnancy before returning to Germany. I was focused; I had a purpose, and no one was going to sway me.

We got to the airport; Ivy was in an ergo baby carrier so that my hands would be free to travel with all of our stuff. I had so many things you would've thought that I was moving back to the US. Mr. Swiss escorted us to the security gate with tears in his eyes. He was joyful for us getting pregnant once again, but sad that I was leaving him.

As I said, bye, I knew this was the beginning of the growth of our family.

I boarded the plane and didn't realize this flight with a baby and by myself, would be a very different 10-hour flight than the one I was on when we arrived in Germany months before. I was alone with Ivy and this was not easy. 10 hours of entertaining Ivy, feeding her, changing her diaper in a small bathroom. The tight space was not the only thing that made me uncomfortable. I was going home to my parents and would have to explain why I left Mr. Swiss behind so I could get pregnant with our second child. I knew this conversation was not going to be pretty because I knew that I was being selfish. By the way, besides my nerves, Ivy threw up on me three times on this flight because I was overfeeding her. I was nervous; I was super tired and unaware of how much I was feeding her. I was standing up shaking her from side to side to put her to sleep, but I think it just given her motion sickness. I was a wreck. I was thankful that I packed a light bag with extra clothes for any emergency. I was wearing a shirt with no bra and my pajama pants when I left the plane. It was the longest 10-hour flight EVER. I arrived in Tampa, and my parents were right there to greet me. They looked at me with a big smile but were concerned about my appearance. They asked, "What happened to you?" I said, *"It was just the longest flight ever."* I just wanted to go home and take a shower!

Getting Pregnant Again

Ivy and I had to make ourselves at home at my parent's house. I knew we would be living there for the next three months or even longer depending on whether the first IVF procedure took. I unpacked our bags, ordered a play yard for Ivy, and hired a nanny and a cook. I had to hire this support team because my parents had full-time jobs and they were unable to take care of Ivy or cook for me. I was concerned about being too active; I wanted to have the best optimal situation to sustain the pregnancy. I was paying for limited stress!

I flew to Atlanta to start my treatment. It was a quick one day trip back and forth. I arrived in Atlanta, nervous but ready to start my physical examine. The doctor informed me about important information regarding the procedure. I was excited to receive the treatment kit. I was ready, and the process was fast and straightforward. I flew back to Tampa and immediately started my first series of estrogen and hormone shots. A few weeks later I returned to Atlanta to undergo the implementation of my frozen zygote. There was nothing for me to do. I just sat there, calm and relaxed. As the two zygotes were placed into my body, I looked at both the nurse, and the doctor and suddenly realized Mr. Swiss was not here. He was not an active participant in the conception of our unborn child. Tears ran down my face. What have I done? How selfish could I be? Why did I decide to be here alone having this baby?

Can you imagine how I felt regarding the realization of my own selfishness? I was adding an addition to our family without my husband's help. Well, he already did his job; he gave his sperm and I gave my egg. Everything was done. The eggs were fertilized, and there was no fun in this! None at all! Just business!

While I laid there I questioned myself. How sad is this? How non-romantic? How selfish? I was nervous, excited, and sad all at the same time. I knew that this was a chance for us to have two kids. I dreamt this. I wanted a boy! What if we have a boy? I flew back to Tampa that day thinking about having a boy! I was excited and ready to continue this adventure of pregnancy.

The next couple of months went by fast. I stayed as relaxed as possible. I made sure that Ivy was filled with joy and laugher at all times. She had an excellent nanny and she was around her grandparents. That was all she needed. Plus, I wanted this baby to STICK! I was waiting to hear the baby's first heartbeat, and I wanted to make sure that the baby developing was healthy before we flew back to Germany.

Mr. Swiss, was back in Germany working long hours and building the business. He missed us, but he had a job to do. He was turning into a workaholic; he couldn't stop because he was focused on making the business successful. Even though he was focused, he took time off and came to Florida for Christmas. Ivy, our unborn baby, and I were excited to see him. He looked tired but happy to see us. We spent Christmas together, and it was heartfelt. I postponed going to the doctor, so we would be able to hear the heartbeat together.

Yes. We were pregnant again!

We looked forward to our flight to Atlanta to revisit the IVF doctor. He needed to examine the baby and me to make sure that we were free and clear to move forward in traveling back to Germany. So a couple of weeks later, we both flew to Atlanta to get word that the baby was fine and that we could travel back home. The doctor told us that we needed to stay in America longer to ensure the health of the baby. Therefore, we stayed until my twelfth week. Then it was time to return home. We gathered our little family and returned home to Germany.

The Return

When I returned home and walked into the house, I noticed a strange stench coming from the home. Then I saw the state of our home. I immediately shouted in shock, "Ooooooh my GOODNESS!"

The house was a mess! Mr. Swiss! What the HELL! He had been living off of pizzas and Apple Shirley's (apple soda)! The boxes of pizza were piled up in the kitchen! There were soda bottles under the couch!
The house was a mess! The house resembled a guy's college dorm room! It smelt like socks and sweaty balls. Yuck!

Holy Shit!
WDF?!

I was angry, but sad at the same time. I realized that he was lonely. He was in despair. I had no idea how messed up he was without me! Where was the housekeeper? Where was the lawn care, guy? Where was his help?

Well, people don't work, if you don't pay them!

While I was in America, and he was in Germany, the distribution of cash became unbalanced. He thought that we couldn't afford the help. I learned later that he had been redistributing the money. After seeing this mess, I went into a fix-it mode.

I panicked seeing the house like this! Although I was very stressed, I kept a smile on my face because I didn't want him to see me sweat. I stuffed my stress inside my belly. He was so embarrassed regarding the state of the house that he dropped his bags and started to help me clean. It was a real big mess. I felt alone at this time even though he was there.

The house felt dark, cold, and it smelled like death. We rolled up the shades and opened the windows to bring fresh air into the home. We walked outside with the 20 plus boxes of pizza, several soda bottles, and Ivy following behind us. My neighbor, of course, came out and greeted me.

She said, *"Welcome back home!"* I said, *"I'm pregnant"* and she said, *"Great!"* Then the next thing she said, was *"There were so many food delivery cars coming to your house, and I was wondering when was your husband going to take out the garbage? Oh, I see now that it was pizza."* Laughing!

I was so embarrassed, by his irresponsible behavior that I became sick to my stomach and that sickness never went away!

This sick feeling seemed to linger forever!

Chapter 8:
The Never-ending Sickness

We can only stuff for so long until we burst.

Valentine's Day

On Valentine's Day, Mr. Swiss wanted to surprise me with a romantic gesture. Unfortunately, I was in no mood to deal with Valentine's Day or anything else regarding romance. I was four months pregnant, and I couldn't bear my never-ending sickness. I was super sick! I threw up every day. I couldn't think; I couldn't eat, and I felt completely helpless. Mr. Swiss thought that sending me a romantic gesture would help me to feel better; but it only made me feel worse.

Mr. Swiss arranged for the local flower shop to deliver a different arrangement of flowers every hour on the hour while he was at work to cheer me up and to show his love for me; but I was a mess. I was the biggest ass on earth. I was laying on the couch feeling nauseous when the doorbell rang the first time. I looked outside of our large windows to see who was at the door. It was a delivery guy, and he was holding flowers.

It's Valentine's Day! Oh my goodness, Mr. Swiss, got me flowers. Oh, how sweet!!

I went to the door and opened it. A cute young guy handed me flowers. He spoke to me in German and told me that the flowers were a gift from my husband. I thanked him, closed the door and went to our little kitchen to find a vase. I was super happy about the bouquet. The arrangement of flowers was so beautiful that it made me smile.

The morning was starting off well, and the bouquet of flowers brought a little sunshine into my darkness. While in the kitchen picking out a vase, I decided to try to eat something, but my sickness quickly returned. Once again, I laid back on the couch feeling nauseous.

Then, an hour later, ding dong. It was the florist delivery guy again. Wow, more flowers. How sweet. Once again, I went to the kitchen retrieved a vase to place the flowers inside of it. Then, I went back to the couch because I was still sick to my stomach. I went from the couch to the toilet.

Another hour passed and then, ding dong. Now I was getting annoyed. What was going on? I opened the door and the delivery guy had a smile on his face. Once again, I went to the kitchen retrieved another vase from the cabinets. Luckily, I had a lot of vases.

Another hour passed by and then, ding dong again. The delivery of flowers continued every hour for the next few hours.

At first, this was fun and I was excited. I appreciated the gesture, but I couldn't enjoy it because I was so sick that day. After a few hours of this, I became so annoyed with the doorbell ringing and me arranging the flowers into vases. At the fourth hour, my attitude changed, I started to complain to myself. I was wondering when this would end because I just wanted to rest. After the fifth hour, I finally realized that this was going to happen until the end of the work day.

Then, ding dong . It was now the last hour of the work day, I opened the door; I was visibly frustrated and now it was a different guy.

I opened the door and the new guy said, "*Ich will das Glück Frau zu treffen, all diese Blumen zu empfangen.*" (I want to meet the lucky woman receiving all of these flowers.) He had the biggest smile, and I had the biggest frown. Long stem roses!! Where am I going to put these?!

I realized that he was the flower shop owner. He came to personally deliver the last bouquet of flowers. I was a mess, and I couldn't fake my unhappiness. I was too sick, too upset, too tired, and just plain frustrated.

Can you imagine, what a terrible, crazy person I was at this time? I couldn't even see that my husband who was working so hard to provide for us and was trying his best to bring romance back in our relationship! It took a year for me to realize that I was a big ass I was that Valentine's Day.

The Farm

Time passed. It was spring. Mr. Swiss' travel schedule increased, and I was still sick. I needed help. I felt alone and I needed a change. Therefore, Mr. Swiss told me that it would be nice to visit his family in the country. He wanted me to get away and experience a different environment. I thought this would be fun, but...

It was in a tiny German town in the Black Forest. The streets were quiet; there were large plots of land separating one house from the other. The town seemed very sweet and serene. As we drove up the hill to the farmhouse, I wondered if this experience would be fun without Mr. Swiss as a translator when he left for his business meetings. I would be a stranger lost in translation. Two older German people were sitting outside waiting for us to arrive. It was Mr. Swiss' Godmother's parents. They had no grandchildren and were super happy to entertain someone from a different culture plus be around Little Miss Ivy. The car stopped, and they came right up and shook our hands just as we barely exited the car. As I looked around, I noticed that there we were on a real farm with chickens. I also noticed that this was not a working farm because the barn was empty. The barn, which was active at one time, now housed cows and other animals. The house was an active bed & breakfast. His Godmother's parents were now retired, had stopped working on the farm, and now only accommodated occasional guests. I noticed that the remnants of a working farm remained and everything was fading out; it was just the couple enjoying the land that they had built on over time. This environment was romantic and sweet.

Of course, in the front yard, they had a Garden Gnome. As we walked into the house, I was greeted by the traditional German decor. The dining room wooden table showed traditional German woodman crafted engravings and the benches attached to the table were thick solid dark wood. On the table, there were crocheted table mats, napkins, and coasters. The room was small with basic fixtures. We went up to the bedrooms and I immediately noticed that there was a sink in the sleeping portion of the room and the shower and toilet were in the bathroom; everything was in a beige, pale pink color scheme. It was super basic. I remember that there was only one TV in the whole house. Oh boy!

They had asked Mr. Swiss to inform me about the food schedule and the menu. Breakfast would consist of traditional bread, cheese, cold cuts, yogurt, and fruit. Lunch would be soup, bread, and salad. Dinner would be bread, cold cuts, and cheese. Oh boy! I thought I would die of starvation. Remember, I had a rough pregnancy. The smell of cold cuts was torture because it made me sick on the spot.

That night, Mr. Swiss informed me that he would be spending the night at the house then leaving the next morning to take care of some business in Switzerland. I panicked knowing that I would basically starve while being in this family home for the next couple of days. I cried that night on his shoulders. I didn't want to be left at this house with these sweet people because I felt lonely. I was very upset that I couldn't communicate with them. I expressed to him that I was afraid of being lost in translation at the house and pregnant. He paid no attention to me and blocked the whole thing from his head. He explained to me that it would be better for Miss Ivy and me to stay at the farmhouse because she would enjoy the farm. He felt that Ivy would not be comfortable driving around in the car with him doing business. Plus, he reminded me that I would get sick in the car due to the winding roads going to his appointments. I would not be able to withstand the twist and turns. So, I decided to stay even though I was uncomfortable. I put a smile on my face, enjoyed the moment and tried to forget about my food situation in the house.

The next day Ivy had a blast! Mr. Swiss had been right. She had an excellent time exploring the farm and being free. I found joy in Ivy's happiness and our hosts' uncomplicated love for one another. I was happy that everyone was happy. A couple of days passed by and yes, I survived! I must say, it was an experience of unconditional love.

<u>Life on the inside of the Silent Cage</u>

We came home, and I realized that I was very lonely. Mr. Swiss was traveling back and forth to Berlin for work. He was fully involved in building up the company, and I felt captured in our home. I felt stuck in my environment and my relationship with Mr. Swiss was distant. I tried to fill this void with the companionship of the moms at Ivy's daycare center. I also built a stable relationship with the neighborhood ladies. I didn't say too much to Mr. Swiss; I just continued to build relationships outside rather than inside of my home with my spouse because that seemed impossible.

Our new baby was growing inside of me, and I was very protective of this growing baby. Because of my previous delivery of Little Miss Ivy, I was considered a high-risk. I met with the OB/GYN every two weeks because of that status. The doctor examined me with a fine tooth comb. I waited anxiously to find out the health and gender of the baby. I didn't want to know anything until Mr. Swiss was available to be there for this important appointment. However, one day I was sitting by myself in the doctor's office and several questions popped into my head. What will you do if this baby has dwarfism or another disability? Do you want an abortion if the child has a deformity? What would I do? Of course, I didn't care if our new child had Dwarfism, but I would feel bad if the child had a mental disability. This was one of my most nerve wrecking doctor visits. After this visit, I worried and wondered if my child was healthy every day.

I was not sure about the health of my unborn baby, but I was sure that I was having a boy; I gave away all of Ivy's pink stuff. I replaced the pink items with blue, green, yellow and white. Finally, Mr. Swiss had the availability to attend a doctor's appointment with me. My doctor met with Mr. Swiss, and myself and she asked, *"Are you ready to see what you are having?"* I was super excited; I knew for sure that I was having a boy. Then, my doctor said, *"You're having a girl!"*

I said, *"What! No I'm not! Excuse me! Check again, the penis is tucked away or small."* She then said, *"No you're having a girl."* I insisted, *"I'm certain that I'm having a boy. Please check again."*

Mr. Swiss, then said, *"Please Timna stop! You will make our daughter a Lesbian or she will have gender confusion because you're stressing!"* I ignored him and continued, *"Maybe he has a small penis. I know I'm having a boy!"*

Having another girl will pull the spotlight from Little Miss Ivy, and cause them to compete with each other. They will always compare themselves to each other. No I don't want another girl!

This was my biggest concern. I worried that my children would be in competition with each other. I worried that Ivy would compare herself to an average height child. I worried that I'd love Ivy less and this baby more. How would my girls react to one other? Would they be a team or competitors?

I was completely concerned and consumed by the unknown interaction of my children. The baby wasn't even born yet and I was stressed. I wanted to solve the problem before it even existed. WDF?!

The fear of having another daughter crippled me. Sadly, this pregnancy was not as exciting as my first. I started to prepare and I rearranged the bedrooms again. The guest bedroom became the baby's room, Ivy's room stayed the same, and the master bedroom was moved to the same floor as Ivy and the unborn baby.

I began to nest again, focusing on my growing baby and Little Miss Ivy's development. Mr. Swiss was only coming home on weekends and traveling a lot between Munich, Berlin, Hamburg, Stuttgart, Cologne, and Frankfurt.

Anxiousness - Mr. Swiss is Missing

The sun was shining, it was a hot day, and Little Miss Ivy was in daycare. I was feeling the kicks of our new baby, and I was in an upbeat mood because I knew that there were only a couple of months to go for the delivery of my new daughter. Something told me to try to get in touch with Mr. Swiss. I called him, but there was no answer. It was strange for him not to answer his phone. I called his secretary, but she couldn't find him and told me that he had already missed several meetings. I started to worry. After a couple of hours, I decided to call some of his salespeople and they said they couldn't get in touch with him either. Several hours had passed and I was hoping that he would contact me. I started to become more and more stressed; I was overwhelmed with anxiety. He was missing. Where could he be?

I walked over to my neighbor's house with my big belly and sat down on her bench. She saw the fear and worry in my eyes. I told her that I couldn't find my husband and maybe something had happened to him. She said not to worry. She thought that I was acting a bit crazy and irrational. She told me that I was worrying a bit too much and that my hormones may be out of whack. Where could he be?

Time continued to slip by and I was beginning to wonder if I should call the police. I was thinking about sending out a tracer on his phone to find him because now it was dinner time and close to Little Miss Ivy's bedtime.

The door opened; it was him. He looked like hell and his eyes were sunken into his head. All I could do was to frantically ask, *"Where were you? I was looking for you all day! Where were you?"* He told me that his phone had died, he had been in several meetings, and that he was sorry.

WDF?! My soul didn't feel comfortable. I was in pain. I knew he was lying to me. He was holding a secret. I was hurt; I felt alone and betrayed. Was there another woman? What was he doing? I was sick to my stomach, and the vomiting became worse.

A couple of months later I would find out what really happened that night.

The Birth

The room was ready; I bought a white crib with all of the fixtures for a little girl. I was ready. Her name is Anavi. The grape to Ivy's vine. I was excited to bring this little bundle of joy in the world. Plus, I was ready to stop throwing up! I was so skinny that my wedding ring was falling off my finger. Can you imagine, I only gained 20 pounds during this pregnancy? I was completely underweight.

Mr. Swiss' mom came to help with caring for Little Miss Ivy while I delivered Anavi. When she arrived, she said the spirit in my house was not right, and that's why I was sick the whole pregnancy. I, of course, fought her on this concept. I told her that the spirit in my house was perfectly fine. I was ignorant, and I had no idea what she was trying to reveal to me. She explained to me that there was a darkness lurking in my home. I thought she was crazy because I knew that I was happy. I disagreed with her and told her that I was unsure of what she was feeling.

It was D-day, the day the delivery day for Miss Anavi. Ivy was so excited to meet her new little sister. She was full of joy to be a big sister. I walked into the hospital, and they said that I had a private room with an extra bed, a full staff, and that I could stay at the hospital for up to seven days.

WHAT? Am I on vacation at the hospital? Am I in the RITZ! I love it!

I was so nervous during the delivery that I shivered all the way to the operating room. I was ice-cold. While they prepped me for the delivery, they ask Mr. Swiss everything about me in German. I was just laying there in awe while he directed Anavi's birth. I felt like I was not in control of my life. I sadly realized that I was relying on him to speak for me, to listen for me, and to plan the delivery of my unborn child. This realization was daunting as I laid in this luxurious situation, I felt stuck and kept. This was the beginning of me truly realizing that I was in a Golden Cage.

It was time and they rolled me into the delivery room for my second C-section. This time I didn't feel like I was going to die, I just wanted to stop being sick. I wanted to deliver this baby quickly to relieve my nausea. I wanted my body back! I felt trapped, confined in my body and soul. I was crippled throughout the pregnancy regarding my diet, my health, my freedom, and my independence.

She came out with force. She screamed! Hello World! I am strong and I am here!

The doctor and nurse were talking in German, *"Sie ist schön, sie ist extrem stark , ist sie Power und sie hat einen starken Willen."* (She's beautiful. She's extremely strong. She is a force of power and has strong will power.)

Anavi was strong like Ivy but different. She had an attitude. She came into this world as a moving force, knowing what she wanted.

By the way, I was still throwing up. Can you believe it I was still sick? WDF?!

Mr. Swiss was curled up with his phone on the roll out bed. He seemed to be in his own world; he wasn't involved with Miss Anavi. He was lost on his phone. I think he was overwhelmed with the conversations and the constant translation of German to English visa versa to the medical staff. He didn't have any quiet time or mental peace. His brain was active 24/7. I didn't think anything of it; I just felt that he needed a mental break.

Miss Ivy came into the room with her Oma (grandmother), and she was super excited to see the baby, *"Meine Kleine Schwester; Liebe sie. Sie ist schön!"* (My little sister; I love her. She is beautiful.) Ivy's diction was pretty amazing at 2 years old.

Little Miss Ivy was ready to change her sister's diaper, she jumped right into her big sister role. She was the big sister. I looked at my two daughters and realized that my fear of competition was unwarranted. They each had their role and I knew everything would be fine. Ivy was a big sister, not by height, but within her heart.

The next day came quickly. I still couldn't eat and Anavi wasn't eating either. She was a stubborn baby. She didn't cry much; she was patient as long as she laid next to me. She had a relaxing spirit. The nurses said that she would wait for my milk to come in. She didn't want to eat; she just drank a little water from a cup. She would not drink from a bottle. Plus, I was in a lot of pain so, I wasn't fighting anything, I had no appetite.

On day three, I had a few visitors, at the hospital and they thought that I was able to eat because I had given birth already. Well, much to my and their disbelief, I was still as sick as a dog. I threw all the food up! My friends had to rush me to the bathroom; I couldn't hold any of my food down. I was embarrassed and sad at the same time. I couldn't believe that I was still sick. Why am I still sick?

I looked at my newborn daughter and asked her why I was still sick. She looked up at me, and I noticed something was in her eyes, a mark. Oh shit! What now?! I showed her eyes to Mr. Swiss but he didn't see anything. I told him that the white birthmark was hidden, Anavi would need to move her eyes around to see it clearly, but it was there. He finally saw it. We called the doctor on-call to show him what we saw and he immediately called a vision specialist.

Why us again? Really? Another problem with another baby! I can't! I can't breathe. I can't. I threw up again. Why am I still sick? Why us again? I can't.

The specialist examined Anavi and reported that the birthmark in her eye was a Dermoid Cyst. The doctor told us that as long as it didn't grow, Anavi would be okay. However, if it did grow, she may become blind in one eye.

WDF?! Are you serious?! Blind?!

At that point I realized that my life is a never-ending dramatic story. I just sat there and cried. I don't want a blind baby. Mr. Swiss was in shock. He was quiet, absorbing the whole thing. He was speechless. I looked at Ms. Anavi, and all I wanted to do was to make sure that she was healthy.

I was depressed and frustrated once again. The only things that kept me afloat were Ivy's smile and Anavi's will power. Anavi waited patiently until my milk came in five days later.

My girls are my rock!

When will this sickness end? I was laying in the hospital thinking that the sickness would never end. 2008 was a mess! If it was not one thing, it was another. WDF?!

2008

1. The Market crashed in the US.
2. We had a house on the market that was not selling.
3. We were under water in Germany because of inflated bills/expenses.
4. Now we would be spending double on diapers and more on other expenses for the girls.

I laid there in that hospital feeling stressed and restless. Thank God I was getting VIP treatment. I got massages and personal care throughout my stay because of my nausea and Anavi's birthmark in her eye. We left the hospital and went home. Mr. Swiss' mother and I could feel the pressure that he was under because he was so distant. Anyone could see that we were underwater and drowning in so many areas of our lives. Therefore, I asked my mother to visit me. She arrived, but she too felt uncomfortable in our home. She agreed with Mr. Swiss' mom that there was a dark spirit in our home. My mom stated to me that she could not live in Germany. She considered Germany a dark country. She thought that she would be depressed because all of her friends were in America. My mom wondered how I was doing it because I had no real friends or support system and my husband was working long hours leaving me at home with two small kids. She truly didn't understand how I could stay afloat.

Thanks Mom but, you're not helpful at all.

That conversation was not helpful or uplifting. My mom stayed a couple of weeks. Although she was helpful in some ways, she made me feel like shit. When she left, I felt worse, but I put on a smiley face. I continued my life with my two kids and my workaholic husband. At least I wasn't throwing up anymore. That was a blessing.

Despite all of my loneliness, I was looking forward to having a Champagne Life. I made the best out of my situation. I loved my babies. I loved the neighborhood. I loved being able to travel without a lot of money. I looked forward to our prosperous future. I envisioned it and dreamt about it. I built a shield, a false sense of happiness, and I loved it. You couldn't tell me anything, especially that I wasn't happy. I made myself happy.

Even though I wasn't throwing up, the sickness was still there. It was lurking and ready to come to a head.

One day, I spent the day looking at the bills and our finance with a fine tooth comb. Things were not adding up. I couldn't figure out where our money was going, why our accounts seemed to be depleted, especially since I was frugal with everything.

Mr. Swiss was arriving home late that night and I waited patiently because I wanted to understand his spending habits. When he entered the house I asked him to explain his use of money that we clearly did not have. I wanted to know about the missing money in our account. He immediately started to cry and revealed to me that he was gambling again. He was very stressed and he needed a means to let it out.

He lost it. He was in despair. He was stressed. He was overwhelmed. He couldn't function anymore under the pressure of his job and the family obligations. He lost himself with the Casino and he lost a large sum of money. I could've killed him!

He revealed to me that on the day when I was pregnant and looking for him, he was with his mistress, the Casino, sitting by the slot machine and gambling his stress away. I thought back and realized that I had not been crazy! I had a panic attack for a good reason because he was hiding and in despair. Can you believe it?!

I was right to be concerned that he was missing! He admitted that he disappeared because the pressure was taking control of him and he could no longer bear it.

I looked at him with all of our bills spread out on the table and I started to cry. Actually, I was in a rage! I was angry! I wanted to punch him! I wanted to f*ck his shit up! I hated him! I couldn't believe he would put our kids and myself in this situation of being broke. He cried and apologized over and over again. I cried and screamed.

Once again my heart was broken into pieces.

This incident happened around the first of November. I was planning to return to America for the Holidays, and this gave me a reason to escape my glamorous nightmare.

So I left!

I immediately purchased airline tickets for myself and the kids; we took the next flight out. He was making me sick, sicker than I had ever been before. I was emotionally tapped out. I couldn't believe it!

He was cheating on me with, the Casino, that slut machine. The Casino, was his mistress and I was hurt. I wanted out fast! Going to my parents' house in Tampa was my quick solution and my medicine.

I quickly realized that both of our mothers had been right. The spirit was evil in our house. It was the devil. The evil spirit that swallowed us up. The fake life we were living of success, when, in fact, we were failing miserably.

Tampa was an escape from my drama. I stayed there for five months to save money and to get away from the pain in Germany. I wanted him to suffer, I wanted him to miss his family and to force him to get help to make a change. I was emotionally hurt and disappointed. My heart was crushed for a third time.

My parents were very supportive during my visit. They played their part by helping me with the kids and allowing me to breathe, to get release from the sick energy that was inside of me. They prayed over me and told me to trust that everything would be okay. I had suffered loss before, and I knew that I could build again. However, I was worried that without Mr. Swiss seeking the help he needed he would deplete our life savings once again.

Mr. Swiss was back in Germany living in the sickness of his stress, silence, and pride. I couldn't help him or do anything because I was sick myself with the reality of his lies and our financial situation. It took me five months, but I made the tough decision, to move back to Germany. I looked at my beautiful babies and decided to take him back. I accepted Mr. Swiss back into my life. I knew he was the one for me and I viewed him as being sick. If someone is sick, you help them to get better. I loved him. Also, it was not just the disease of gambling he was fighting but, the sickness of silence.

It's Time to Get Healthy!

Chapter 9: Champagne Anyone?

It always tea time when you have the time

Two years passed and we were on full throttle, kids, life, the business, the relationship, and saving to increase our financial situation.

The house in Atlanta sold. The gambling stopped. The business was flourishing. We were back on the up-and-up. It was champagne time!

I developed incredible friendships with people who had similar lifestyles. It seemed to always be champagne time. The husbands of some of my friends traveled just as much as mine; so we had time for exercising, lunches, playdates, shopping, and of course we drank champagne.

The kids were in daycare, and I had my life back. My mornings were for me. I had a glimpse of freedom. I decided to get my body back in shape. I was working out, running, and getting my confidence with my physical appearance back. However my soul was still hiding heartache and sadness.

My friends were my foundation. They gave me advice; they were there for when I needed a laugh, a shoulder to cry on, or help with birthday parties for the girls. I needed to forgive Mr. Swiss, but instead, all I did was push my issues under the carpet and lived a rich woman's marriage.

<u>The Secret to a Rich Girl's Marriage</u>

1. Lower your expectations regarding your spouse coming home and giving you attention.
2. Accomplish what you need to accomplish for your kids and yourself without waiting for your spouse because he may not come home.
3. Hope that he will find time for you and the kids.
4. Don't allow yourself to be broke down.

5. Make sure to look divorce ready - meaning physically attractive to others.
6. Understand that you're getting older so some cosmetic procedures may be needed.
7. Schedule dates with your spouse, through his secretary or you will never see him.
8. Make time for your relationship outside of the kids.
9. Oh, don't worry about special occasions if he misses it. You do you!
10. Always have great friends around you who are just as financially successful and understand your glamorous pain.
11. Make sure your children are educated, cultured and confident in their walk.
12. Don't let your kids see you sweat.
13. Don't f*ck up your money.
14. Stash your cash for a rainy day.
15. Be a 'Trophy Wife' - men are simple.
16. Have fun!
17. Don't forget to always manage your home.
18. What he doesn't know won't hurt him since he is always gone.
19. Plan all vacations, travel and get out.
20. Keep the house busy, then you won't get depressed.
21. Keep focused on the end goal (It's different for everyone)
22. Don't accept less than you deserve.

I lived by this code of honor. These 22 rules were my commandments. I kept afloat by following these commandments because the love was fading and the business of the relationship was growing.

Divorce -Ready

After a while, I realized that I was working out and my body was still not looking exactly the way I wanted it to look. I needed more. My boobs look like they belonged to an old lady. I needed a change. I didn't want Mr. Swiss to touch my breast because they were droopy and lifeless. They looked the way I felt some days. So I decided to make a significant change to my breast which I never thought I would ever do. The holiday rolled around again and I went to Tampa to ask my mom about my deflated breast and what she thought about me getting breast implants. She saw my breast and she said, *"Oh My Goodness, your breast look older than mine!"* Right then and there I knew that I was going under the knife!

I saw a cosmetic surgeon in Tampa. I walked in the office and there were young women sitting waiting for their turn to get a consultation. Where am I and how did I get to this point? The receptionist asked me to fill out some documents. The first paper was a financial obligation that included a payment plan. This was college all over again. I felt like this doctor was cheap and it was an office that appealed to lower income clients. Where am I? Am I a stripper who is here waiting to get bigger boobs? Wait a minute! I am not a stripper. I felt violated in some respect and cheap. I felt alone even though Mr. Swiss was there. He was in shock as well.

The doctor entered the room. She was an African American woman with a pleasant smile. I will call her Dr. Smith. Dr. Smith started the consultation by showing us pictures of different breast sizes and informed us of the different procedures to achieve the best results for my body. She asked me what I was looking for and then she asked Mr. Swiss to leave the room. She made him exit the room so that I could share my truth. Before Mr. Swiss left, he looked at me with confusion as to why he couldn't be part of the decision making. I was also a bit uncomfortable with this. But, she was right. Why do I want the influence of a man on my body? It is my body. However, for a quick minute, I did feel that, as my husband, he should be a part of the consultation.

During the consultation the doctor was super sweet, but there was one thing that was off with her; she didn't seem meticulous. She retrieved a bra from her desk and gave it to me a bra to try on. I noticed that the bra was dirty. I couldn't believe that she would give me a sample bra and implants that were dirty. The implants and bra were given to me to illustrate what the weight and measurements might look like on my body. I was reluctant, but I tried the sample bra on and used different size implants in it. However, I was disgusted. Then, she gave me a t-shirt. I decided right then and there not to use her because the t-shirt was also dirty. It had makeup all over it. Yuck! Can you believe that both items were dirty? I'm a meticulous person, so I immediately questioned her cleanliness. Why would I allow someone who doesn't care about the sample bra/clothing that she gives her potential clients to handle my actual procedure? Yuck! I walked out feeling like I needed a shower.

Nope. Not her!

I walked out of her office with some useful information. This information was fun for both Mr. Swiss and me. She told me to go to a strip club, look at other women's boobs, touch, and feel to determine what was right for me. She asked me to ask the women questions about their procedures. What implants did they use gel or saline? What was the weight of their implants? Where was the incision? Was it under the muscle or over? Mr. Swiss was super excited about going on this adventure. This was the start of exploring our creative sexual side of life. Why Not? Live Life 4 Real (smile).

<u>My New Addition</u>

I started to feel that time was running out on my life. I was getting closer and closer to 40, and I become concerned about my appearance. I wanted to get my boobs done. I decided to search for the best female cosmetic surgeon, and I found her in Germany.

My German cosmetic surgeon was the best!

I walked into Dr. K's office in Frankfurt, and her office was like walking into a high-class gallery. Everything was in either gray, black, or white. The office was posh: luxurious, but at the same time, classy, sleek, immaculate, and she presented herself in this same fashion. She didn't have many patients at the time because she had just started her practice. She wanted the best for herself and her clients. It was love at first sight. I knew that she was my doctor.

Dr. K made sure her clients felt like a million dollars. She held a high-level confidence in her work. She was concerned about me and wanted me to get exactly what I wanted. She didn't influence me in my decision. She just educated me on the best procedure. She was also concerned about my level of comfort. I told her that I wanted to stay in the hospital overnight because

I was scared. She made it happen. She also used the best technology. Dr. K knew that I rather spend more money on my comfort, education, and security of the procedure, than spend less money for a quick fix.

It was a success!

One day after the procedure, Mr. Swiss looked at my now perky breasts and said, *"This was the best investment we ever made."* It really was one of the best decision that we had ever made. (LOL) Yes, it was the best investment we ever made because our sex drive went up. I got my sexy back and he knew it. However, sex was still not passionate. He was still a workaholic, and was not emotionally there for the family. I think this was when my role of the Trophy Wife became more of a priority for the both of us.

Recklessness

The new boobs and the new outlook on life made me reckless. I wanted to party more, drink more, and be in the party scene of Frankfurt. Some of the ladies that I was hanging out with were young and vibrant. I was missing something in my life and it was apparent. I was missing fun, excitement, and a purpose. I was bored.

You may say that I was going through a midlife crisis.

My babysitters were making money. I had at least four of them on call. I found time to run free at all times. I was working out in the morning, having lavish lunches at noon, playing with the kids in the afternoon, and partying at night. I even had champagne on the playground. We had a bottle wherever we went. While the kids played we drank from our wine or champagne glasses. I was living the Champagne Life.

The girls had my full attention despite my drinking; I focused on their education and their well-being. They were involved in several activities such as swimming, ballet, and skating. They learned how to ride their bikes super early without training wheels. They became independent quickly. When it became dark, I tucked them in their beds and I was out.

To increase the romance in our relationship, I started to travel to Mr. Swiss' office to meet him for lunch. He was happy that he could be free from the burdens of fatherhood and business for a little while. He had his woman back. I was paying attention to him and stroking his business ego. I was his cheerleader. Therefore we started dating again.

But...Something was still missing! Passion!

Sex was still missing. He was still not taking care of himself. He had a foul smell from his mouth because he was not taking care of his teeth. He was not drinking enough water. He was eating fast food and his body and soul were deteriorating. He had no energy to satisfy the intimate part of our relationship because he was focused on work.

One weekend I went on my first ski trip with friends. We were in Switzerland skiing and living the high life. Well, my friend's husband is a powerful business lawyer, and he requested that I get a sexy, handsome male ski instructor with great teeth and a perfect smile. We paid for the 'perfect' man to teach me how to ski. #dangwhydidwedothat?

Yes, this is how the 1% lives.

Order what you want. All you have to do it pay for it.

The sexy ski instructor and I were alone for hours. It was the whole day, and he saw the lack of passion in my eyes. He was speaking my language of the need for satisfaction. I swear he could've f*cked me right then and there. I was a hot mess! I was craving intimacy, passion, and desire. It was written on my face and he could read it!

Mr. Swiss surprised me by arriving early at the mountain top. I was so mad to see him! At that point, I realized that I had fallen out of love with him; but I couldn't admit that to myself or him. I was a mess!

My eyes and body language showed my disappointed in seeing him. Something came over me. I couldn't stand the sight of Mr. Swiss. As we went down the mountain on the Gondola, I sat there in silence and my mind was flooded as I looked at Mr. Swiss with disgust and disappointment. I felt guilty for not loving him. Plus, I knew that I was ready to do something with someone else with the right opportunity. He had f*cked my situation up by coming up to the mountain early. I knew, he knew, and the ski instructor knew it. It was the craziest and most awkward unspoken situation ever.

I wanted the ski instructor. I wanted to be free to do what I wanted to do without regret! I didn't want to be around him. I didn't want anyone to know that this was my husband. I didn't care for him. I immediately hated him. I wanted out! I wanted to ski away with someone else. I was disgusted with myself for being with him.

I started to question my relationship.

Why am I with him? Why am I here? Why don't I leave? Why do I feel like I want to cheat? What is going on? Why don't I feel attracted to this person that I call my husband? I realized that I was missing passion! I needed to feel the lips of another man on my lips. I wanted to feel someone else inside of me. I needed and wanted more. I didn't feel a sexual or emotional connection to him.

I'm trapped!

We got down from the gondola, and as we walked away, the ski instructor asked me if we wanted to join him and his buddies for a drink. I said, *"Of course!"* I didn't want to end the time with him. I wanted to be on a date with someone else other than my husband. Mr. Swiss face was in a panic. I knew he was like, WDF?! I bet that he wanted to slap the shit out of me in his mind. I think he was shocked to see me like this, flirtatious and not giving him the time of day. I was disrespecting myself and him all at the same time and I didn't care. I felt reckless and I loved it. It was a thrill. I was high and ready to go on a ride.

Mr. Swiss dismissed his feeling of me wanting someone else. We just partied, got drunk with his buddies, and left.

We returned to the hotel and had sex, but all I could think about was having sex with the ski instructor. Mr. Swiss was a tool at this point to satisfy my desires of being with someone else. I knew at this moment that I had also fallen out of love with him sexually.

I felt reckless!

Mr. Swiss and I hadn't had a real emotional intimate sexual relationship for years. I realized that we hadn't kissed or made love since living in California. We were not aligned emotionally or sexually. Having sex was a job, it was not enjoyable.

OMG!

I was sexually frustrated and I needed a release. Going to a strip club or erotic environment was not good enough anymore. I need more from him but, he couldn't satisfy me because of his stress level at work.

The Affair

So time went on, maybe a year or so, and I knew something was still missing. I didn't want another child. I was missing passion in my life. I was missing a sensual touch and love that a man would give me. Being a Trophy Wife was not sustaining my love for Mr. Swiss. I loved him, but I felt like I was losing myself in the process.

I gardened, ran more, detoxed, and stopped drinking. I was finding myself again. The kids were in school; the days became longer, and lonelier. My friends started to go back to work. I was alone. I felt unneeded in my role. So, I looked for job opportunities in Germany, but I was fearful of being trapped in Germany with a man I didn't love in that way. Plus, Mr. Swiss was dragging his feet on requesting a visa from his company to allow me to work.

I felt trapped in my world.

One day, I decided to hire a company to repair my landscaping. The owner of the company rang my doorbell and when I opened the door something electrifying happened. He introduced himself and once I shook his hand, it was all over. A jolt came over me. I looked and noticed this tall, manly, broad-shouldered, guy with reddish blond hair that was short and brushed forward. Mr. B's hazel eyes pierced, my soul. The jolt went through me, and I felt like I had an out-of-body experience. I noticed that Mr. B was very attractive and had a sense of mystery. He started to introduce himself to me and as he spoke, I noticed that his accent was not that of a typical German man. Mr. B was speaking English with an unfamiliar German accent. I went blank for a second while Mr. B held my hand. It seemed like there was no one around us. Our energy immediately connected.

WDF?! Wow! This had never happened to me before.

I was so confused. I couldn't understand what I just experienced. All I knew that it felt good. It really was the strangest thing ever. While I was showing Mr. B and his crew the area that needed repair, Mr. Swiss arrived in his mini coup. I thought he would take over and finish the conversation with Mr. B; but he didn't. He told me to continue the conversation. Mr. B then asked if I could go with him to the store to pick up some materials. I then told Mr. Swiss to go to the store with him and he said, that I should go since he had to return to work. So, I got my purse and jumped into his rugged green, Jeep that had a fantastic sound system. While we were driving, I was so intrigued with his Jeep Wrangler. I knew this going to be my next car. I loved Jeeps, especially Jeep Wranglers. I asked Mr. B to explain the sound system in his bad guy car. What was his favorite music? He immediately started to jam all of my favorite Hip Hop songs.

Who is this guy?

Mr. B told me that he was a part-time DJ. As we were driving, I became immersed in the sounds of the music and in his energy. I was also surprised to meet someone who was into the same music as I was. I knew that we would be friends. Plus, I was planning Mr. Swiss' birthday party, and I needed to hire a DJ. Mr. Swiss' 40th birthday party was months away, but I knew that I wanted to have a big party celebrating his special birthday.

The drive seemed endless. While driving, we quickly got to know one another. When we arrived at the store, we talked and talked. On the drive back I noticed that we were in the car for longer than on the way there. I said, "It's *taking us a long time to get back?*" He said, "*Maybe I got us lost for a second so we can continue talking.*" I thought that was super cute. I knew I needed some attention and I was eating it all up. As Mr. B drove me back to my home, I knew that he would be in my life as more than a hired worker; he would be a friend.

I went into the house and left him to prepare for his project. I walked into the house and, when I looked back, I saw that he had the biggest smile on his face. It was so charming. I couldn't stop thinking about this drive, our conversation, and our handshake. It was such a crazy feeling. I had the chills and a smile came over my face as I watched Mr. B and his crew discuss the project outside of my window. My windows were large, and I could see Mr. B peaking inside. I felt like a beautiful bird in a golden cage looking out at the world.

My longing for home and my sadness at not being myself fully comfortable in Germany crept up on me again as I sat quietly by myself. I missed NYC. I missed my home. I missed my zone. I missed myself. I missed my soul. I missed my place. I missed my culture.

While I was going through my sad thoughts, Mr. B rang my doorbell again to ask a question and I came outside to talk about the landscaping job. As we talked, a feeling came over me; this guy felt strangely like home. There was an immediate comfort level that I hadn't felt in a long time. I was missing something and I needed something new. I went back inside and started to make a meal for the girls, and all I could think of was this feeling of home and comfort that I was missing.

**Shit! Shit!
What is going on? Why do I feel this way?**

I tried to fight the feeling, but it continued to linger in my mind and body. The next day, I wanted to see him again. Over the next few days, he came to the house to work on the landscaping project. We would smile, but not talk. He would look at me through my window as I worked out, prepared meals, played with the girls, and lived my life inside the house.

One day Mr. B came by himself and invited me to his birthday party. He asked me if I wanted to go to a fitness studio with him since he saw me working out each day alone in front of the TV. He suggested that I workout with others in a group to get out of the house. We started to spend time together at the gym. We did yoga and other exercises while we got to know each other better. We went on lunch dates.

Then something that was supposed to be innocent became something more. We developed an emotional connection. We called each other everyday and we texted throughout the day everyday. I became addicted to the attention that I was getting that I hadn't been receiving from Mr. Swiss.

It was time for Mr. B's party. Mr. Swiss accompanied me to the party and I had a blast. I found out that my crush was an excellent DJ. He was also an excellent dancer. He danced like he was from NYC actually like he was Black in another lifetime. His friends were from diverse backgrounds and his parents were super cute. I was in my element.

This only drew me closer to him.

I was planning Mr. Swiss' party with Mr. B's help. He made himself available to find the singer, to go over all the music, the food, the cake and the party logistics. Mr. B. became part of my life. I didn't need to drink or feel lonely anymore. I was regaining my emotional confidence. I was on a high for life. I didn't even think about leaving Germany. Mr. B was always around me.

I was having my cake and eating it too.

Mr. Swiss was ignoring me and my need to be emotionally connected. I expressed to him several times that I was lonely and that I was missing something. I started to be less vocal about this as time passed because I felt unheard. Mr. Swiss and I were having sexual intercourse at this time, but it was not passionate, it was like a job. I was not into him or the sex. Mr. Swiss and I also spoke on the phone everyday; but, something was still missing. The spark was not there. He thought if the home/finances were fine, everything was fine. However, the opposite was happening. I was not fine. I needed some attention. I craved it. I needed intimacy and joy in my life that I was not getting at home.

The intimacy I craved came directly from my new friend who was now in my life. The candle was lit in my heart. The fire inside of me was burning. He was my spiritual connection; I felt like he was an angel that was sent to lift me up. He freed me from my Golden Cage. This person who came in my life made me feel free.

We started a love affair. My crush became my Lover.

First, there was the KISS. His lips against mine were like a magnetic field. I kissed guys in the past before Mr. Swiss which was okay and my first kiss with Mr. Swiss was special. However, this time the kiss was different, it was electrifying. It was like a jolt hit our systems. He even said to me that he never kissed anyone like that before. I thought the same-thing. A kiss is so simple but can be so divine. Our lips were touching and our tongues locking. It was so smooth, so soft, and so sweet that the hairs on the back of head stood up. WDF?! We didn't want to stop kissing; it felt so good. I was melting.

I was melting inside and out. My heart was captured by another. I was freed briefly from my cage; but I wasn't free. I felt captured with no way out. He was inside of me. It felt golden. The golden wand was inside of me. I felt like singing. My song was soft in my heart. It felt good. He taught me things that I never knew about my body and how to express love through tantric lovemaking. He gave me exercises to do to increase the muscles of my vaginal walls. He taught me how to release and let go during the act of lovemaking. How to experience the ultimate orgasm. I taught him how to release dominant creativity, how to unleash his animal, and how to increase his drive to be successful in business.

I had no idea, how deep I was into this situation. It was crazy. Months later, Mr. B asked, "*Do you want to leave him for me?*"

It felt good. It felt right. But it was so wrong. I knew that he was not the one for me in regards of a life partner. He didn't have the abundance of money because his business was young. He was still living at home in an apartment downstairs from his parents, and I knew he would want a family of his own. I had no desire to have more children, or to get divorced or remarried to the unknown.

Divorce was not an option for me. I was 100% sure about that because my neighbor was going through an ugly separation which left her kids confused, her husband an emotional mess, and everyone in pain. I couldn't subject my family to so much pain. I was not that person. I'd rather die with a lie. I'd rather enjoy this moment of intimacy. I knew it wasn't going to last. It felt good. He felt good. He felt like home and his kiss felt like heaven. It was not me anymore. I was someone else. I was simply addicted to Mr. B.

The Party

It was a surprise White Party for Mr. Swiss' 40th Birthday. I was excited that the music was ready, the venue rented, and all my friends invited. Yes, it was all of my friends, because Mr. Swiss had no friends of his own at the time, just work colleagues (subordinates) who were my friends.

We stayed at a beautiful hotel and, his mother, hidden in the room next door, was waiting patiently. He had no idea that I had planned a surprise White Party with the theme, **Welcome to Miami**, because that's where Mr. Swiss went when he first arrived in in America. I had a photographer, live band, DJ, American food with a Swiss flair, a Cabaret performance, and 40 invited guest. It was the party of the year.

Mr. Swiss was shocked, and surprised that I had his party at his favorite restaurant. He also was super surprised that his mom and our kids were there. We danced the night away.

But the irony of it all was the cake. I was dead on the cake. Let me explain. I had asked the baker to design a cake with a brown skin woman laying on the top that was sexy in a bathing suit and a debonair man sitting with a gun; it was supposed to represent James Bond in action. However, the cake was not what I ordered. The brown skinned woman (me) was actually dead; James Bond (Mr. Swiss) had killed her (me).

I was dead on the cake

The symbolism of me dying on the cake represented the death of our relationship. I t also represented his anger towards me regarding the affair, which I so desperately tried to keep a secret.

The Secret Came Out

We were making love, and I was enjoying it way too much. He said, *"Wow, tonight you're so into me. You even want to kiss me. But I feel like you are not making love to me. I feel like you want to make love with someone else, not me."* I looked over at Mr. Swiss and told him that he was crazy and that I was just feeling him; he was my desire. He was who I wanted; but he and I knew that this was a lie. I was lying about my desires for another. We went to sleep that night, and the next morning our worlds collided.

It was a dark morning because he woke me up in the middle of the night, upset. In the 12 years of our marriage, Mr. Swiss trusted me and that night he woke up in distrust. He had checked my phone and checked my emails because he felt something was not right. The truth came out about me meeting my Lover while he was on a business trip to Portugal. He exploded and an angry interrogation began. He wanted to know everything when, where, how, and why! He questioned me all through the night, all through the morning, and all through the day. He wore me down mentally for three days until I revealed the truth regarding this love affair. My nerves were shot! I still refused to tell the full truth, just a glimpse of the actual reality.

I was trying to save myself and my relationship even though I was the cheater, the liar, and the adulterer. I kept the lie. I told him that it was just a kiss, it was only an emotional affair. He wanted to believe and I wanted him to believe my lie. He became the Devil in the home, he hunted me down, stalked me, and watched my every movement for months. I kept the lie and the affair going through all of this madness. I was addicted to the kiss, the feeling, the intimacy that I had longed for months before. The torment of Mr. Swiss drew me closer to Mr. B because I was under pressure and I didn't want to stop. I was now getting negative attention from Mr. Swiss. This attention was not healthy; it made me sick; it was stressful and draining. I was watched and stalked. I hated it. This behavior continued for years afterward.

The pressure and stress wore me down. I stopped calling, texting, and hanging out with Mr. B. It started to fade. It was too much. Being watched and stalked caused me to be anxious. We both could no longer bear the stress of the relationship. I needed to give my attention to Mr. Swiss. I allowed him to control me. He demanded my attention. I convinced myself that it was okay because he was my children's father, my husband, my provider and I was guilty. I felt trapped. I could not have my cake and eat it too. I couldn't give two people the attention that they deserved. I decided to deny intimacy for security. It was over. The last text we sent each other was the symbol of the scissors. It was cut.

Stressed about the breakup, I laid there in my room and cried. Mr. Swiss was traveling in San Francisco and I got a late phone call from my mom. She was crying, and she stated to me that my father had committed the ultimate sin; he had an affair. As she cried, I cried because I realized that I am my father's child. I was living the same lie he was and now it was all in the open. The betrayal that my mother felt, I felt for Mr. Swiss. .I cried. I was sorry. I was guilty. I was weak. I hated myself for the stress that I caused my relationship. I laid in bed for a couple of days. I dropped the kids to school and picked them up late. I just stayed in that dark room realizing what I had done and where I came from. I told Mr. Swiss of my pain and sorrow. I revealed to him my family secret. I was guilty.

Mr. Swiss said he would forgive me and he told me that he ran across the Golden Gate Bridge so that he could release his stress. He loved me and he knew why I cheated on him. He also wanted to talk to my ex-Lover so he could have a full understanding of why this happened and where he fell short. He wanted to have a conversation with the man, who captured my emotions and stole his wife. He wanted to find peace with all of this and move on. But did he?

Mr. Swiss said he forgave me for my betrayal as I forgave him for his. We were equal. Were we?

Berlin

A couple of months went by, the holidays came and went. It was a new year, a new season, I stuffed my feelings from my past relationship away and tried to make it work with Mr. Swiss.

Mr. Swiss wanted to explore our sexual side and increase the intimacy in our relationship because he knew that we were missing this. We started to be more sexually risqué. We were needing and wanting more intimacy, the sexual intimacy that was dormant in our relationship for years. So we decided to create a new life of sexual exploration.

Mr. Swiss researched sexual exploration and introduced it to me. He wanted us to explore the world of sexual fantasy and exploration not with other people, but with each other. I knew I had a large curious, sensual, sexual appetite with my now ex-Lover; I didn't need this new extreme fantasy sexual relationship, but Mr. Swiss did. I became a willing participant. He wanted me back, so I submitted to his desires of wanting to explore his sexual side. I was excited that he wanted me and needed me in the bedroom again.

Mr. Swiss travel to Berlin often and he knew of the sexual scene in Germany. He investigated and researched where and when to go to explore the sexual unknown. He wanted more and wanted to explore. One evening, I met Mr. Swiss at his job and he wanted to go to a lingerie store, and there they told us about the Official Berlin Sexual Fetish yearly party. I, of course, asked if this was dangerous and if people were actually having sex with each other. WDF?! What is a Sexual Fetish Party? They explained that it was a party where people go to explore their sexual fantasies. You do not have to have sex with anyone. People are polite, dress in costumes, masks, or are just plain naked. Some are tied up; others arrive as a couple or come with friends. This party was a big deal.

I was excited but a little nervous about the whole thing. Why not explore? This was not love. This was not sensual. This was pure sex. This was pure sexual fantasy. Sexual misconduct. Sexual mischief. Sexual exploration. We both knew what we would be getting ourselves into, or did we?

It was almost time to attend this Sexual Fetish Party. We had to buy outfits, tickets, and prepare for this trip of sexual exploration. We ventured back into the lingerie shop. It was on a quiet street, a small boutique in Frankfurt. The ladies that owned the shop were two larger women who had a sense of class and mystique about themselves. They were very well versed on sexual pleasure toys and male/female lingerie. I was so excited about being educated on what to expect and what we needed to wear for this sexual exploration.

As we walked through the store, one of the owners gave us some great ideas on what to wear. I wanted to be classy with a touch of sexiness in black. Mr. Swiss wanted to be a bit Dracula-like, all in black with a bit of leather and a bit naughtiness added to his outfit. My dress was a see-through black lace gown that hit the floor. It was sexy and classy at the same time. It was also super expensive. Mr. Swiss decided to wear a cape with a pair of leather briefs.

We were ready!

The day arrived and we took the two-hour train ride to Berlin. We stayed at a luxury boutique hotel waiting for the party to start. We were super nervous but excited about this exploration. The time seemed to go by so slowly.

Now it was night and the moon was shining brightly. Our outfits were ready. We jumped into the cab. Mr. Swiss, of course, put on some black jeans and a shirt because he was too afraid to walk out of the hotel looking crazy. I wore a jacket over my long dress.

We arrived at the large club. Many people on the line entering the club looked conservative. However, I also noticed that they were carrying overnight bags and small pieces of luggage. It was our turn to go through the doors. They asked for ID and if we had anything that we needed to put in a locker. A locker? Genius!

We entered the club and immediately started to people watch. It was a sight to see. Everyone was changing into their costumes or the lack thereof. The coat checker took our items and as he walked away, I noticed he had no bottoms and a large cock. Oh shit! This guy had an incredible asset. I guess he was showing it off (smile). I shook my head in astonishment. By the way, this guy was about 60 years old. He had no shame in his game. Now I was super curious. What will we experience beyond the coat check and the locker room?

We walked deeper into the club. Oh my goodness! We were in Sodom and Gomorrah. Where the hell am I? In Hell? This is crazy! WDF?! I decided to be a bit more open-minded and stop thinking like a school girl. I realized that no one was drinking because people wanted to be clear-headed on what they were about to do. There was no drugs, just plain freaky people. I looked around and noticed that there was a guy tied up with someone whipping him. I was shocked.

Oh boy! There was this beautiful athletic African woman who was wearing a skin tight, bodysuit. She accompanied a White male, most likely a banker, dressed in a dog collar. She was pulling him. Hmmm... I think this was a dominatrix situation. Wow! I could get into that.

The club seemed to resemble a theatrical theme park. I quickly realized that this was not a swingers club. It was a club for eroticism. It was Cirque de Soleil - Zumanity in Vegas, the movies, *Eyes Wide Shut* and *50 Shades of Gray* all in one. It was the craziest SHIT ever. It was a theater of actors and actress performing.

Then the show began and latex was the theme. The Puppet Master on stilts entered the room; the strings were hanging down attached to two people. A sexy, gorgeous and athletic guy dressed like a puppet connected to a sexy lady who resembled a doll walked through the crowd. It was a sight to see. The theatrical make-up on the performers was a masterpiece. I felt for a moment like I was at the opera. The Master of Ceremony was covered in latex, a latex Barbie. Could he/she breathe? Is that a girl or guy under all of this latex? This person was covered by so much latex that he/she could have been the CEO of one of the largest company in Europe for all I knew. The mystique of the whole thing was incredible. I just knew that the majority of the people in this club were wealthy. I felt like I was in one of Madonna or Lady Gaga's private parties.

Now I will not lie to you; there was some kinky shit that I'm not mentioning in this book. I had my mind blown with some of the things I saw. It was freaky! We continued to walk around; we played the role of the sexy couple intrigued by others and their sexual fantasies. I'm not going to lie; we were excited to see the sexual escapades of others. We were voyeurs in a world of mystique and lust.

Did this help with our sexual desires towards each other?

Yes, it did! We left the club, full of excitement and a willingness to explore our sexual boundaries. We made love that night. We felt like we were 20 year-olds again. It was exciting and intriguing. We made love finally! It was good. It was sex. It felt like heaven. It felt risqué. We went all night. We traveled back to Frankfurt the next morning. While on the train ride back home, something came over us. We were like young lovers; we wanted to make love and we wanted to do it on the train. So we slipped into the train's bathroom and had sex. It was the most erotic thing ever. I was excited, I was in love with my man again, he was the one for me, and I was the one for him. Our passion was growing, and we were in love again. After having passionate sex in the bathroom of the train, something came over me.

I felt dirty and guilty.

I had to tell him the truth about my ex-Lover and our love affair. I knew if we were truly going to rekindle our love romance he needed to know the truth. As tears ran down my eyes, my emotions flooded my soul. I felt guilty. I had to tell him. I wanted to tell him. I told him the truth. My soul had to tell him. I had to get it off my chest. My Lover and I had sex. It was not only a kiss; but we made love.

He got mad. He started to cry. He was done with my bullshit. He was upset. He was mad. He was done. I cried and told him I was sorry. I f*cked up! I made a mistake. I just had to tell him.

It was over!
It was done!

Chapter 10:
The Big Move

It was time to say goodbye and welcome something new.

That was it; Mr. Swiss was ready to move back to the US to leave all this drama behind. He wanted me far, far away from Mr. B. I was confused about my feelings for Mr. Swiss. I was also still confused about my feeling for Mr. B even though I hadn't seen him in a while. I knew we needed to move and start a new life without the cloud of my affair. Mr. Swiss loved me and I loved him but in a strange, sick way. Neither one of us wanted to release control of the relationship. We loved how we looked around people, what this meant to our kids and family. We had a business arrangement, less love and more business.

Our form of intimacy was more sadistic than sensual. It was a power struggle.

<u>The Move</u>

We sat down and came to the realization that we needed to move. The girls' schooling was difficult. It was hard for me to assist them with their German and English assignments. I wanted to start working and Mr. Swiss needed to keep control of his home and business. It was inevitable. We were moving back to the US. This decision was swift; it happened so fast. We started to plan for our departure.

That summer, we went to Chicago, NYC (Brooklyn), and Minneapolis to figure out the best city to start new our new life. The kids were active participants of this big decision regarding the city that we would eventually call home.

They were excited. Our first stop New York City. My extended family lived there and many people that I loved lived in NYC; but, the girls didn't feel comfortable. They thought the noise of the city seemed like people were dying or unhealthy. I didn't want either the girls or Mr. Swiss to be completely stressed because of the craziness that NYC had to offer.

Our next stop was Minneapolis, where Mr. Swiss' best friend lived. This state was more relaxing, but I felt like it was a bit too Vanilla. I needed more diversity; I wanted to be able to find a job that I would allow me to grow and embrace my diversity in the workplace. The kids were excited about moving, and they didn't truly have an opinion about Minnesota but one day during our trip my Little Miss Ivy asked, *"Where are the brown people?"*

Chicago was our next and final stop; we all loved it there. It was beautiful and welcoming in the summer. The kids had a blast, and Mr. Swiss could do business. Plus, I had amazing friends in the city. However, we thought about the winter months for Little Miss Ivy. She wouldn't be able to handle the harsh temperatures of the city and feel comfortable. Plus, I couldn't withstand the winter months. I didn't want snow.

We were flying back to Frankfurt, and it hit us on the plane. Atlanta! Why not Atlanta? Ivy said, *"Yes Mommy. Wasn't I born there? Let's go back to Atlanta where it all started."* Atlanta here we come!

During the next year, we planned our return to the US. Mr. Swiss and I were doing well. We went out on dates, rekindled our relationship and were ready to move on.

However, you know, there is always a but in this relationship.

Time went by super fast; the planning stages of the move took no time. We were ready to go! The moving company came and packed everything.

The house was empty, and everything was looking up until the landlords came to review the home. Oh my goodness, this was a mess! The landlord and his wife were the Devil; they wanted to nitpick every detail. Can you believe that they wanted us to return the house the way it looked when we rented it seven years ago? We had to pay to repaint the interior of the house, add fresh landscaping, and repair the carpets. I couldn't believe it. They wanted to screw us and they had the right to because we gave them permission seven years ago. We signed an agreement to return the house back to its original condition not knowing that we would live there for seven years. WDF?! It was like throwing money out of the window! Just crazy.

While we were waiting for the school year to end, we moved into a small two-bedroom apartment. During this time, our relationship seemed to get better. We had a friendship, but not as lovers, as roommates. The sexual escape died, and we were back to normal, a semi-sexless marriage. Even when we went on several vacations without the girls, there was no physical intimacy. We had lost trust. Our relationship was business as usual.

He silently hated me as much as I hated him. We were trapped in this fake relationship that we had created. We moved back to Atlanta and quickly realized that this was the best thing that happened to us as a family.

Change.

We rented a white ranch style home on a hill with a large drive up, a big grassy front, and a back yard. The bedrooms were all on one floor. This was the first time that we were so close together. The house was not as big as the house in Germany, but it was exactly what we needed to help our family to form a lasting bond.

We decided on an environment that would be kid friendly. They could play outside in the huge back yard. The elementary school was diverse, and the people were friendly. It was what we needed.

I remember sitting outside supervising the delivery of our furniture from the moving truck. My neighbor, an older White lady in her 70's, came out to ask me, *"Who are the people moving in?"* I said, *"I'm the person moving in."* She looked shocked. Welcome to Georgia! (LOL)

After we had unpacked, I knew that this move would be different. We would build a new foundation for our family. I thought this would be a great opportunity for me to start contributing financially to the household. However, for some reason, Mr. Swiss was apprehensive about me pursuing any endeavors outside of the house. After a few months, I started to get restless. I wanted more for myself than taking the kids to school, talking on the phone, cooking, and cleaning. I decided to go against Mr. Swiss' wishes and do everything that I had been dreaming of or wanted to do and was unable to do while living in Germany. I was releasing his control over me. I decided that we were in a business relationship and that our love was what it was: RETIRED. My job was the girls and to be the Good Wife.

I made a list and began working to check off items.

- Volunteer in the girls' school.
- Be the main support person for the girls; find their passion and involve them in activities.
- Get on an executive board in the community.
- Volunteer in the community.
- Educate myself by taking some enrichment classes.
- Find my passion.
- Get another Master's Degree or a Certification.
- Start networking with women entrepreneurs.
- Find dates for my friends.
- Build a reliable community.

My New Adventure

I decided to start my new adventure with something that I had dreamed of since I was six years old. I wanted to be a marriage counselor, image consultant or something of that nature. I wanted to help people to be the best they could be. I thought about these careers because deep down inside I was seeking answers for myself and my relationship.

I went to several different conferences seeking the best career avenue for my new self. I wanted to break out of this role called Mom/Housewife and do something for myself. So, I went to an image consulting program. They looked like me, fabulous, classy, and well-dressed; but they didn't have the depth that I had regarding counseling the inner person, not just outer. I needed another program; so I found a coaching program online. This program was more in depth. It was a longer program than the other. IPEC, the life coaching program was 18 months compared to many other life coaching programs which were six months or even several weeks online. I wanted something more in-depth so I could be credible. Once I further investigated IPEC's program, I knew it was something that I had to do.

I was speaking to a friend at the time whom I trusted and told her of my interest in coaching and my passion for helping people. She immediately put me down and said, *"Why would someone pay you for your advice or coaching? You need a Doctorate or a Master's in Counseling."*

I questioned myself. I had self-doubt. So, I went to Mr. Swiss about my thoughts regarding this coaching certification compared to a Master's in Counseling. We had a long discussion, but when he challenged me, serious self-doubt welled up. He was against me rather than supportive of my efforts.

He challenged me with a series of questions: *"Are you sure this is a good program? This sounds expensive. What job can you get when you have this license? How would you handle the day-to-day schedule with the girls? How would I handle the duties of the household?"* He then shared his travel schedule with me and it seemed very busy.

We continued our discussion and all he could do was come up with more questions: *"Where would you find the time to get this done? Where will you find the money? What about the kids? What about the home? What about my needs?"*

I was filled with self-doubt. I became nervous. Once again, I felt trapped in my role of being a housewife and a mom. I didn't feel supported. He had no solutions, just a pile of obstacles for me to try to overcome on my own.

I felt trapped in a role that I had created. I wanted out! I felt trapped in my marriage. Why was I feeling this way?

I finally told myself to wake the f*ck up! I wanted to live the life that I wanted to live and live it 4 real. Thank God I had other awesome friends to help me get out of this rut and find my truth. My best guy friend told me, *"Timna, you can do anything you set your mind to. You are only trapped because* *you have made yourself trapped. Go get that certification and the money will come."*

Thanks for Angels. I decided to schedule the introductory class; it was a whole weekend. I asked Mr. Swiss about his schedule and if he could help with the girls. He said, started in with more questions/obstacles: *"Why are you so selfish? Why can't I go with you? Why didn't you invite me? I saw that you could invite another person for free. I wanted to do this with you. I wanted to learn about coaching. It will help me in my business. Why are you so selfish?"*

Excuse me?! Really?!

I walked away so upset about him not wanting me to do something on my own. I didn't understand. Why is he was saying that I am selfish for wanting to do something for myself. I became super defensive about taking the course. After all, I had stopped working because of him. I opted out of my dreams because of him. I decided not to go back to work because of him. I decided to be the sole support person for the girls because of his schedule and him. I moved to Germany because of him.

Excuse me?! Really?! Are you serious?!

We started arguing. Mr. Swiss, repeated his concerns. This was the start of him being competitive and breaking me down emotionally, verbally, and spiritually. This argument would not be the first time that he would struggle against me accomplishing something outside of the home and not solely for him.

He became angry. He became competitive, non-supportive, and wanted to make my life hard. He wanted to pay me back for cheating on him and giving my love to someone else. He became my silent enemy. He hated me, but loved me at the same time. It was the start of my spiritual battle with the man I called my husband. This silent battle lasted for years to come.

It was the weekend for the coaching course; I was excited and ready to embark on my new journey. However, Mr. Swiss was stressing me, *"Why are you going to the conference? The kids need you. I can't handle the kids. How long* will you be? Why don't you stay home? Why not drive to the conference each day so that the kids won't miss you? It is too expensive. You will miss the kids. The conference is in the same city why stay in a hotel?"

I had to look past his stressful and manipulative words and PUSH FORWARD. I told him crying, "*I will find the money. I will put everything on my credit card. I will hire a nanny to assist you over the weekend. I'm only five minutes away; I can come home if there is an emergency.*"

He stressed me. I already had low self-esteem. I was a f*ck-up! I was a mess. My nerves were fried. I became anxious.

However...

I was ready for my new adventure!
I needed to cut the umbilical cord!
It was my time to shine!

That weekend, Mr. Swiss kept texting me. He had several manufactured emergencies. He made me feel very stressed out; but I had to ignore him. This program was very intense. They dug deep into my psyche; I allowed this to happen because I made myself the guinea pig in class. I knew that I needed emotional help; but, I had no idea how much help I needed. The class was eight hours each day for three days, and we had homework each night. The class had people of all ages and all walks of life. Many people took advantage of the opportunity to invite a non-paying guest to be part of the class for the first weekend. There were about 25 people in this intensive and thought provoking private class.

The course allowed us to question our world and the people around us. We were forced to be open up and to think deeply about our lives: how we saw the world and how the world saw us. I was blown away by this experience because I allowed myself to become vulnerable and allowed the instructor to coach me in front of the class. This was the most dramatic, explosive, and vulnerable thing that I have ever undertaken. I was NAKED and EXPOSED in front of strangers.

He brought me in front of the room, and I sat down. Anyone could challenge me and ask me questions on how I thought about myself and the world around me. It was cool, but there was one question that I had to delve deeply to answer with the naked truth: How did you feel in Germany? I said it out loud because it was my Naked Truth. I shared it with these strangers. In Germany I had felt like I was 60% less of a person. Me? Timna? 60% less of a person?!

The sad truth was that I really had felt this way. I felt 60% less of a person and I had low self-esteem. I lost myself in Germany! I couldn't believe it. Who had I become and who was I now, a wife, a mom, a housewife?

I felt like I was nothing and I had achieved nothing over the last ten years. I had followed my husband around and denied myself what I wanted which included being successful in the business world, being an awesome mom, and being loved.

This was a shock to my system!

Right then and there I signed up for the rest of the coursework to become a Professional Life Coach. I knew this was not only about me helping others, but it also about me helping myself.

I came home after this extreme experience. I was a hot mess. I wanted more; I wanted to learn more about myself. I wanted to find Timna again outside of this relationship and my role as the housewife.

Mr. Swiss was not as excited as I was. He was frustrated with my new joy. He was upset that I had homework, that I had to coach people, and that I had to work.

I told him that I needed the office in the house to work and that he could have an outside office since he was traveling so much, I needed to set up shop for my new endeavors of being a life coach. He was very apprehensive and this was not good. We started a silent battle over space in the house.

I knew that I wanted to move to a bigger house, I thought this would help with the feeling of being crowded or with the battle over office space because this was putting a strain on our relationship.

During this time, my mind was occupied with passion which allowed me to find joy and peace. Mr. Swiss was traveling, and when he was gone, I made mountains move in regards to my coaching, the girls, volunteering, networking, and the home. I was a happy superwoman. When he returned, there was always a struggle over space, criticism, and extra work.

My Family

My family visited and this was a bit of a strain because our relationship was not in a good place. When my family visited, my emotional workload increased because I had to juggle their expectations, the needs of my children, my endeavors, and Mr. Swiss' need for attention. It was always the hardest thing for me mentally and spiritually. There was always a battle of attention from everyone. I kept a smile on my face, but usually, by the end of the visit, I would feel irritated, stressed and overwhelmed. I would need a vacation for myself. My relationship became more unhealthy and dysfunctional during this time. We became more distant when my family visited than closer. My family came first, and I was mentally exhausted. At the end of the night, I had no energy for him or his needs.

My core issue was that I didn't know how to say no. Also Mr. Swiss didn't say yes, I can support you.

I didn't know how to say no to them and their expectations regarding me doing everything, (cooking, entertaining, cleaning, and taking care of their personal business). I needed to say no to them to save the little bit of relationship that I had left.

I went to bed tired and I woke up tired.

My family didn't understand my frustration and my need to say no. They just kept on taking and taking until there was no more to take. I was just done. I allowed this to happen because I didn't clearly express my frustration. They also didn't understand my exhaustion because I wanted them to feel good. However, Mr. Swiss knew my stress level by my irritable personality. However, instead of trying to provide support and balance, he took on my emotions and became irritable as well.

Two irritable people will result in a lack of communication, distance, and resentment.

By the way, my parents thought I had a bad spirit in my house. Yes, there was a bad spirit which was silence, stress, and tiredness, lack of empathy, emotional distress, and resentment.

Even though we were tired and stressed we still went out on date nights and enjoyed ourselves outside of the home. The date nights allowed me to let my hair down and have conversations with Mr. Swiss. I needed these moments just to recharge and to allow myself to give him the attention that I felt he needed.

I was constantly giving of myself and no one was giving anything back to me.

One Night

One night a couple of months later, I needed time alone, to sleep, not to think, but just to relax. I needed a weekend off from my life. So, I decided to have a mom staycation at a hotel in the city of Atlanta. The staycation was something that I did twice a year to regroup and recharge since I was giving so much of myself at all times.

The first night of my staycation, I asked Mr. Swiss to come to the hotel so that we could have a fantasy date night. He would pick me up from the bar and we would make love upstairs in my room.

I was super excited about this. I had dinner at the bar. I was wearing a sexy dress with no underwear so it would be more enticing for him when he saw me. I was ready to have our sexual rendezvous.

After I had eaten, I ordered a Cosmopolitan (like in the movies) and I texted him to see if the sitter had arrived. Mr. Swiss then texted me that he was a bit tired. I looked at the text in disappointment. I was ready; I had red lipstick on, a tight dress, and no panties. WDF?!

Excuse me! What is he doing? I'm ready!

I looked at the bartender, and he saw the look of surprise on my face as I read my phone. He said, "A pretty lady like yourself, is being stood up?" I said, *"No. I think he's still coming."*

I continued to drink my Cosmo in hopes that Mr. Swiss would change his mind and still show up. Well, he did. He surprised me and came. However, at this point I had been sitting in the lobby waiting so long and that I had started to feel a little sad. So, I told him we should just go straight upstairs.

As we walked towards the elevator, I thought he would embrace me or make me feel special, and that did not happen. He was distant.

We entered the room and with the king size bed, I was ready for him just to f*ck me. But he was still a bit distant. I asked him what was wrong. Then he told me that he was tired. I told him that I understood; it had been a long day for both of us. I asked, "Would you like to leave?" Mr. Swiss said, no, I want you.

I was ready! Then we started to kiss. The kiss was distant and uncomfortable. It was completely off. So we decided to start to make love and that was just awful. We knew that this was not a match. We were not a match.

I started to cry.

Mr. Swiss, looked at me and said, *"What's wrong? I knew I shouldn't have come! I wasn't into it! I can't do this!"*

Then, he left.

That night, I laid on the bed and I cried. I cried all night. I kept crying until the next day. I stayed in the room and cried.

I couldn't believe my situation.

He couldn't love me!
He didn't love me!
He didn't want me!
Is something wrong with him?
Is something wrong with me?

I called a friend, and I told her everything, and we both thought about what was going on!

I realized that Mr. Swiss and I were not in love anymore. We just were friends. That night he couldn't make love to me, and it hurt me to the core. I couldn't breathe all I could do was cry.

What kind of relationship is this?

I later discovered that Mr. Swiss had a deep fear inside that my going out represented all hell breaking loose and that I would be cheating again. He had no trust in me and so he could not give me the true intimacy that I wanted.

The next night I decided to hang out with a friend and go to a club. While I was waiting for her, I decided to be reckless. As I stood there waiting for my friend to pick me up, another friend called me. She was pouring her heart out about the lack of intimacy that she and her husband had. She was also in a biracial relationship. She was wondering if all white guys stop having sex with their partner when they are stressed. She was talking my language. We laughed and cried about our men, having a low sex drive. She said she was going to get a lover. I did that before in Germany, and I honestly didn't need to do this again. There was no need for me to seek a new lover. But, I'm not going to lie, I thought about it. I laughed with her, told her that I would just blog and fantasize about making love to someone else.

I want to be wanted by someone else.

I didn't tell my friend about my conversation with my girlfriend over the phone because I knew she wouldn't understand. I just wanted to go out and have fun. I didn't want to think about my troubles or rehash them with anyone else. I just wanted to have fun and feel sexy.

As we went out to the club, I realized that I could dance and have fun with someone cute that I didn't want as a lover. I didn't want to act on my feelings; I just wanted to have a good time dancing. I wanted Mr. Swiss to want me. I just wanted my relationship to get better.

After a night of hanging out, I came home and thought to myself. Can Mr. Swiss and I figure this out and find intimacy with one another? Should we get risqué again? What can we do to regain intimacy even if it wasn't perfect?

I just needed positive attention. The Naked Truth was that this relationship was a business relationship rather than an intimate relationship. We needed to seek counseling in order to find a way to build back trust and intimacy.

I started to blog deeper, to share my emotions about our relationship, because this was my way towards healing. I was in a coaching class, finding myself, coaching others, being a mom and wife. I needed a release of energy and blogging was the best way to do this. The blog was a major stress relief for me, but my words sometimes caused pain for Mr. Swiss. He saw my pain, read my words, and thought he was going to lose me. He thought he was going to lose the person that I was, the quiet, less vocal, completely committed to the relationship trophy housewife. He saw my eyes bright and the light on my brain shining brighter. He was unsure of what to do with my voice. He was nervous that I wanted to branch out and find myself again, the old me who was confident, active, an activist, and a feminist. He didn't want to accept that this was healthy rather than reckless. I didn't want to be that person who has silenced herself anymore. I was drowning and my blogs were my life jacket.

<u>**The Excuse**</u>

Both Mr. Swiss and I were avoiding each other. His traveling increased so it took him away during the week and he came home on the weekends. I was focused on staying busy with the kids, their activities, and my passion for expressing my voice.

The months flew by fast. During the week Mr. Swiss was MIA, he didn't give me his travel schedule until the last minute. I had no idea where he was staying, how long he would be gone, or even what city he was visiting. I would repeatedly ask him to send me his schedule and to provide me with his flight details and hotel information. He refused, ignored me, or just simply sent it when it was convenient for him. I would see pictures of him on social media at events and only then did I know where he was. His lack of communication caused me to become over anxious. We only spoke once a day or not at all. He would call me when he was around people, and he would always be in a rush. He was living a secret life.

At first, the lack of communication made me grow suspicious of his actions and his whereabouts. I started to have dreams of him in dark alleys wandering, without purpose or focus. These dreams occurred more and more frequently and caused me to become paranoid and stressed about his secretiveness.

I had panic attacks because I wouldn't know where he was. I was again in a situation of helplessness, like Germany, afraid of being alone and not having a cushion with the kids. I suspected that he was deliberately trying to drive me crazy because of my past infidelity. He had not forgiven me; he was punishing me. The girls would come into my bed at night, knowing that I was sad because I was unsure where their dad was traveling.

They would ask me, "Where is daddy?" I would reply, *"I don't know? He is not answering his phone."* Then they would fall asleep with me in my bed. This was driving me crazy!

I felt stupid. He was making me feel stupid!

I was making myself crazy!

I was done! His communication was distant and I started to respond in kind. I became distant and less concerned about his travel schedule.

I started to build my community of friends and business acquaintances. I made friends with some of the parents of my childrens' friends. I became rebellious with a purpose. I wanted to get out of my cage and have wings of freedom. I decided to join women entrepreneur organizations and clubs. I went to many events, stayed busy, and became active in the community. I didn't want to be a housewife who was constantly worried about her husband anymore.

I was relaxed, and I didn't allow him to stress me out over his lack of communication. I decided to pull up my big girl panties and Live Life 4 Real without him.

April Fool!

Months passed. I told Mr. Swiss that it was important for him to kiss another person because he had a lack of intimacy and was disconnected from his passionate side. Deep down inside I wanted him to experience the passion that I experienced with my lover. I didn't want him to miss the opportunity to experience this for himself with another person even if he was not able to experience this with me. I had no idea that he would take me up on my offer and kiss someone else or how I would feel about it.

Mr. Swiss traveled to NYC for work and I didn't think anything about it nor did I worry. He was there very often, so I didn't think anything about him meeting up with friends. He sent me a picture of him hanging out with a good friend of mine who was also married. I was cool with it. I said, *"Have fun. I'm going to bed."* I thought nothing of it. I even forgot that I previously suggested that he kiss someone else to experience passion with another person.

The next morning, April 1, 2014, I took the kids to school. I was nervous about going to an appointment for my first mammogram. I was terrified. I was stressed, wondering if they would find something or if everything would be fine. As I was driving to my appointment, I received a phone call from Mr. Swiss.

He said, "I'm sorry. I am so sorry. I'm sorry for making out with your friend last night. I feel like shit. I'm sorry."

Excuse me!

I yelled, "What the hell are you telling me? I need to go into this appointment. Did you know that I am having one of the most important examinations of my life? My first mammogram and I'm terrified. My stomach is killing me and you're calling me with this shit?"

Why the hell would he call me about some stupid shit right before I go into the office for my mammogram? Didn't he know that this was one of the most nerve wrecking things a woman can experience in her life? What the hell was he thinking?

As I drove into the parking garage of the medical center in disbelief about what I was hearing, I tried to stay calm. However, I was not calm in my soul. I told him in a very calm voice, "You're disrespecting me by even calling me and telling me this story right before my appointment. I can't listen to you right now. I will hang up this phone and move forward with my day because this is stupid." Then, I hung up.

The parking garage seemed so dark and small. I got out of my car to enter the building and all I could think about while waiting for the elevator was that this must be a joke. After all, it was April Fool's Day. Maybe he is playing a prank on me. This is an April Fool's Day joke.

The elevator doors opened and the phone rang again, this time it was my friend calling. I answered in a joking voice, because I knew this was a joke, "Hello beautiful!" How was your night? Did you have fun with my husband?" She then asked, "Did he call you?" I said, "Yes, he told me that you guys made out last night. So, did you have fun?" She was shocked at my response and said, "How do you feel about this? You did tell him that he should kiss someone to *feel passion."* Wait! I said, *"Yes, I did tell him this."* She then proceeded to tell me about the events of the night. I was shocked!

WAIT… This was not a joke?
WAIT... Excuse Me!
WAIT... She is serious!
WAIT… They made out!

WDF?!

I was so f*cked up! He is trying to drive me CRAZY!

I was now at the front desk of the doctor's office. The receptionist told me to fill out some paperwork. She noticed that I was nervous. She heard the tremor in my voice. I just blurted out *"I think my friend and my husband are playing a joke on me because they each told me they made out last night. I'm sorry! I'm in shock. Sorry, let me hang up this phone and fill out this paperwork."* I told my friend that I would call her back after my mammogram.

I couldn't believe what I was hearing. I was confused. Are they playing an April Fool's Day joke on me?

As I was filling out the medical forms, I decided to call my good guy friend, so he could help me make sense of this nonsense. I told him the events of that morning and was curious about his thoughts on the situation.

He said, *"They're joking! It's April Fool's Day. Relax Timna; it's a joke."* I told him, *"I'm stressed about getting this mammogram. I'm in the room preparing myself, and this was not funny! I do not have time for jokes."* He then told me, *"Timna, relax you're always overreacting."* I said, *"I can agree with you but, this time, I feel like this is not a joke, and I'm sick to my stomach with nerves."*

After my mammogram, I decided to call my friend back to find out if they were playing a joke on me. She said, *"No. I'm sorry, but it's true. I made out with your husband, and I'm sorry!"*

Oh, my GOD! I flipped out! I became overheated. I had a panic attack.

What was I hearing?
What did he do?
What was he thinking?
What was she thinking?
WDF?!
WDF?!

Then she proceeded to tell me the about their rendezvous in explicit detail. It made me sick; it made me stressed. I had no idea how to react. She had no idea how stressed I was because I kept calm and said nothing. I was in shock. I hung up.

As the day went on and the phone rang constantly.

It was her.
It was him.
It was her husband.
It was my best guy friend.
It was my best girlfriend.

I was going crazy!

The questions, the answers, and the drama. It was all unbearable.

It was time to pick up the girls. I drove to the school, parked the car, and told everyone on the three-way call that I could not talk anymore. I was getting the girls. I had to put on my game face; I had to pull up my big girl panties for them. It was game time.

I said with my best mom smile, *"Hi girls. How was school today?"* They both answered, *"Great mommy! How was your day?"*

I wanted to say!

MY DAY WAS TERRIBLE...
GOD DAMMIT, THESE F*CKING PEOPLE ARE DRIVING ME CRAZY!
I CAN'T BELIEVE MY F*CKING DAY!

But…..

I smiled and said, "*Oh, I had a great day!*"

Then, the phone rang again. It was her husband and her on a three-way!

WDF?!

I told them, "*I'm in the car with the girls and I can't talk right now!*" They would not hang up. Her husband wanted to know if they f*cked! What was the truth? She wanted to get my forgiveness and assure me that they didn't have sex! I was scratching my head about the whole damn thing!

I didn't give a f*ck! I just told myself the worst thing that could happen is that they f*cked. Oh well! They f*cked! Let me off of this damn phone to be with my girls.

F*CK THIS SHIT! I don't care!

So the conversation continued back and forth! Mr. Swiss was added to the discussion as well. What a big hot mess! The girls noticed me getting agitated and then I almost got into an accident. This was one of my most stressful drives home! The husband also asked me a ridiculous question. Did I want to have sex with him since they made out?

WDF?!

This is not a swingers club and I'm not a swinger!

I asked, "*Are you serious?*" Yes, he was! Anyway, I ignored his dumb comment and tried to finish out the day with my girls. I decided not to accept any more of their calls and avoid the whole damn thing for the rest of the night. After I had put the girls to bed, I called a girlfriend of mine to tell her the story, and she immediately started to cry. She said, "*Timna why aren't you crying?*" My exasperated response, "*Cry for what? This whole thing is some bullshit. I have no time to cry!*" She went on, "*Aren't you hurt that your good friend betrayed you and you can no longer have this friendship with her because the trust is broken?"*

Oh my goodness! This hit me like a brick! I can no longer speak to this person because the trust has been broken and they both may be lying to me. Oh shit! I have been betrayed. At that moment, I realized how Mr. Swiss had felt when I told him that I cheated. The tears began to flow, and they did not stop. I cried and cried. I could not stop.

Mr. Swiss came home that night. I was angry, afraid, and sad about what my feeling towards him would be. He ran into the room to embrace me and said, *"I'm sorry. I am so sorry. I didn't sleep with her. I swear I didn't sleep with her. I'm sorry. I am so sorry."* As the tears ran down his face, my tears dried up! I was done!

I was in an I-don't-give-a-F*CK state of mind!

I just want us to be together because I knew I had done the same thing. I cheated so why couldn't he make love or have love from someone else? Why was I being selfish?

So, I told him that I accepted his apology and it didn't matter to me if he had sex with her, what mattered was that I could not trust her. I had lost a friend. This was a friend that I spoke to everyday about my life, including my relationship. She was my confidant and I thought that I was hers. I was so mad at the fact that he shitted in my pond and I could never go back in it because it was now dirty. It didn't matter what they did, how much they did, or even how long. I didn't care about the details. I just looked at the disrespect and lack of trust that I now had for the both of them.

Would he continue to see her when he traveled?
Would she tell him all the things that I said about him?
Would she throw me under the bus?
Would he now feel the need to have an affair?
Oh SHIT, what have I done?

These thoughts flooded my mind for the next few months. I had no trust for Mr. Swiss or her. I was immersed in my feelings of distrust and he became more distant and less thoughtful about my feelings. During this time, we were friends by day and roommates by night. We pushed our resentment of each other under the carpet and was living life like nothing happened. I placed myself into a silent cage.

Dancing in the Rain

Chapter 11
The Storm

If you think the storm is over, watch out, another one might be lurking in the dark.

2015

A year had passed, and during that year, we stopped talking about our problems and started to live more like the passing wind. We shared joy, laughter, went on vacations, smiled and took pictures for the world to see how happy we were. Yes, we were happy during the times we were together experiencing life, but we were being passive aggressive. At any moment and at any given time, we were arguing or saying terrible things to one another. We were passing like the wind and sometimes there were storms and there was rain; but most of the time there were clouds with a little sun peeking through.

February 2015

It was girl time and my bestie planned a girls' trip to Puerto Rico and I was on board. I was ready to let my hair down with my friends and be free of the nonsense at my house. My excitement came to a halt. It was bad news; it was really bad news! Mr. Swiss' mom suddenly passed away! Oh my goodness. WDF?! She is in her 60s. What is going on? He is now without parents and our kids are now without their grandmother? What do we do now? Do I still go on the girls' trip? Do I stay home?

Oh shit! Now he is really going to be a needy stalker and irritable volcano waiting to erupt. I am so f*cked!

I didn't want to be insensitive, but should I ask him if I can go on this trip? As I sat there consoling Mr. Swiss, I knew my flight was in the next couple of days and I really wanted to go. I was nervous about his response, but I knew I had to ask, *"Can I go on this girls' trip? Do you need me to be here? Should I cancel? What do you want me to do?"* Mr. Swiss told me to go because there was nothing that I could do. Everything would happen when we traveled to Switzerland in a few weeks and he would be okay.

I was jumping for joy inside, I knew I should've stayed with him to mourn his loss, but I really wanted to go on this girls' trip. I needed the release. I needed to selfishly regain my emotional strength because I knew that the funeral would be tough on Mr. Swiss.

It was the day of the flight, and I asked him again if I should cancel. He told me, "*No. Enjoy yourself. Just be near a phone in case I need you.*"

I got on my flight and immediately knew that I was going to have a fun time. I forgot about everything that was happening in our house and focused on the freedom of being with my friends on an island. I was running away from my problems and it felt good.

During my trip, Mr. Swiss revealed to me that he had several other trips that he had already booked before the untimely death of his mother and he needed me to accompany him.

So my schedule for the next six weeks became: week 1-Puerto Rico (girls' trip); week 2-Mexico (business trip); week 3-Switzerland (family to the funeral); week 4-Rest at home; week 5-Singapore and Hong Kong (business trips).

Mexico

It was time for Mr. Swiss' annual business vacation trip to Mexico. This time, it would just be him and me, no kids. I knew we were still at war. We boarded the plane and as we approached our seats, Mr. Swiss went straight to his window seat without stopping to help me put my bags in the overhead. Another man saw me struggling and assisted me. Mr. Swiss was not my husband; he was a selfish stranger boarding a flight.

I asked Mr. Swiss if I could sit by the window since we were not with the girls and I hadn't been in the window seat in a while. He said in a harsh tone, "*No!*" The older white lady with gray hair seated next to us in the aisle seat just looked at me and shook her head. I knew she was thinking, *"How the hell did I get seated next to the angry couple?"* I looked at her and said, *"Sorry."* Then, I looked at Mr. Swiss and said, *"Really are you going to be an ass on this flight? You get to sit in first class all the time. You get upgraded all the time and you have the window seat all the time."* He said, *"Exactly! I fly all the time and I need to be comfortable. You don't need to be comfortable."*

Mr. Swiss went on to say that he felt I was not appreciative. He said that I was happy when we went on trips and dinners, but did not love him or show affection towards him. He wanted more hugs, more affection. He went on to say that I had been more affectionate prior to having kids. He said that I was a better wife before the kids. He resented having to take me on a trip that he had won with his hard work and effort at his job. Again, he felt that I was taking advantage of rewards that I had done nothing to earn.

I could only respond with silent. Mr. Swiss did finally offer me the window seat. However, at that point, I didn't even want to be in the seat I occupied. The flight was very uncomfortable; we silently hated each other all the way to Mexico.

After the plane landed, we both knew that it was 'show time.' We needed to leave our argument on the plane and forget our problems to move forward. So we did! We pulled our big boy, big girl panties up and started fresh when we got to Mexico. We were such good actors that no one knew we were having problems.

Several days later we even forgot about our problems and had sex. The sun and the sea water seemed to wash our problems away and allowed us to be romantic again even if it was just for a moment.

Then he said something stupid again.

Man! Will it ever stop?
This is exhausting.

We were with a friends in Mexico at their special place and we decided to play a word game.

What is one word that describes you?

I said, *"Intuitive"* and Mr. Swiss responded, *"Silent."*

Silent?!

I was done. I knew that word. Mr. Swiss regularly used Silence to punish me. Silence was my kryptonite. That word destroyed me in so many ways. Silence had also crippled my soul.

I was so upset in my spirit that the fake love faded away quickly. I was so ready to go back home and see a counselor. I needed to see a counselor fast! I was going to break down and die a slow death inside my soul! I was not listening to my intuition screaming. What is wrong with you Timna? This guy is a mess. I didn't say anything to Mr. Swiss. I stayed quiet and drank a cocktail.

I decided to stop fighting for the relationship. I was DONE and I knew it.

It was time for us to return to Atlanta and back to our routine. I was wondering what would happen next. What will be the next turn of events that will prompt another argument or outburst from Mr. Swiss? I became even more distant and distrusting of his reaction towards me. Mr. Swiss felt my distrust and saw my distance.

A week later....

Mr. Swiss sent me an email with his concerns.

> Here is what I want!
> 1. I want to be supportive of your goals.
> 2. I want to keep you clear of extra unnecessary work.
> 3. I want you to be safe.
> 4. I want you to be trusted.
> 5. I want you to be free.
> 6. I want you to be independent.
> 7. I want you to have a helpful husband at home.
> 8. I want you to be a professional woman that doesn't feel she is held back!

9. I want you to feel that your husband (me) is understanding.
10. I want you to feel sexy around me; selfish thought maybe, but I haven't made it clear lately that you are very hot and sexy.

I may have not all the answers on how to do this to its fullest... The above are not pretty words; they are my true feelings on what I want. I do not know why I keep on sending you an opposite message, but my intention is just that. I don't want to lie and say I understand your anger towards me... What I do understand is my intention and my action are not aligned, and I want to make it an effort to do the right thing going forward. I am reaching out to a group that might just help me to get there, but I ask for your support.

I love you.

I did not answer his email, and I did not answer his calls because he knew all the right things to say, but his actions were the opposite. I thought this email was manipulative, and I did not trust him.

He then sent me a follow-up email after I finally sent an email with an Action GIF with President Obama. Yes, let's have action. We have been talking so much, but we had no action. This email sounded great, but, I knew that nothing would change. So, I had sent a silly email with the word Action on it.

Mr. Swiss:
Your behavior, however, is making it very impossible for me to get there. Your response and you not picking up the phone makes no sense and is completely distrusting. Are you cheating? I open up and you beat it down... Why?

Yes, why was I beating him down? I did not trust him. I didn't want another guy. I just wanted him to love and respect me truly. I was tired of our core issue being swept under the rug, and being in a silent war against each other. I knew he said that he wanted to make the relationship better, but I was unsure.

Mr. Swiss saw that I was drifting further away and he was worried that I was cheating on him like I had in the past. He quickly made an appointment to see a therapist. This was a shock to me. However, I also knew this was a bit of manipulation and a strategic action that he was implementing to save his investment, me.

Singapore and Hong Kong

Walking through the airport of Singapore, I noticed the silence of the people, the whispers of their voices, and the fast-paced movement of their feet. The airport was a symbol of our fast paced life and the silence that we had for each other's pain.

The first day in Singapore, I was super excited about being in Asia, and I wanted to experience everything that Singapore had to offer. I started to plan my adventure without regards to Mr. Swiss because I knew he was working. I didn't want to stay in the hotel. I wanted to explore the region and I thought he would be excited about this, but he wasn't.

I told Mr. Swiss of my quest to venture out and experience something new each day and he seemed completely disinterested. He was consumed by his own thoughts. On the second day, after breakfast, I ventured out on my own to explore the city. When I returned to the hotel, I was excited to share my adventures. He, on the other hand, immediately was aggressive and stated: *"While you were having fun, I needed to work. What do you think this is, a vacation?"* I became quiet, stared at him in astonishment. Mr. Swiss was so nasty in his words that the way he was speaking to me broke my heart. He didn't want to hear about my day or my whereabouts in a foreign country and he did not want to share anything about his day. He was just silent. I felt like shit.

I now know that Mr. Swiss was grieving and couldn't handle his grief. He really should have cancelled the trip and dealt with his mother's death. The stress of work and the loss of his mother devastated his world. He was lost and angry. He felt that I was not there to support him, but because a trip to Singapore and Hong Kong was on my bucket list. He was very wrong.

Over the next few days, we went to breakfast, went to dinner, and barely talked. I tried to figure out what Mr. Swiss wanted me to do and how he wanted me to support him. I was actually very aware of his need for attention and I was treading lightly making sure that we would sightsee together. I tried to make the best of our time there. We did exciting things in Singapore, but the looming feeling of loneliness hung over my head like a storm cloud.

After Singapore, we went to Hong Kong. I was still very conscience of his emotions. I asked him to give me a schedule so that I could be around him when he needed me. I wanted to be available for him because I didn't want him to feel like I was having too much fun during the time that he was at work. I also didn't want him to blame me for any mishaps on the trip.

These two weeks seemed to last forever because the silence and him blaming me for everything was hurting my heart. When we walked through the city, he would walk faster than me. I felt like I was always trying to catch up and he was walking away from me. It felt like I was symbolically holding him back. He didn't want to wait for me or protect me. I also felt like he wanted us to get into something that was reckless, and I was fearful of his need to do something risqué.

In Berlin, I was ready to explore and get crazy, but in Hong Kong, I felt dirty and lifeless. I did not want to be a part of anything dark and risqué. The funny thing is that he never actually asked me to get into anything risqué on the trip. It was just a gut feeling. Mr. Swiss stayed on his phone late at night, hiding his search for something risqué. I felt in my bones that he wanted and needed something more than I could give him. I actually think he was mad that I was there with him. It was the strangest thing ever. I felt the darkness around me, but I didn't speak to him about it.

During our stay in Hong Kong, we were around one of his colleagues and this made everything a little bit more relaxing because that person was a good distraction from our painful situation. Despite our unspoken anger/fear, we went to amazing places, ate at fabulous restaurants, and experienced the culture.

At night, my soul was telling me something while I slept. My dreams became more vivid and scary. The most replayed dream was of Mr. Swiss walking through dark alleys lost in his thoughts, wandering and looking for something risqué. These dreams made me sad and stressed that I was living with a person who was suppressing his feelings. I took on his pain and made it my own. I also became silent in my silent cage worried about his reaction to any inquiry or comment I might make.

I cried the whole 22-hour flight home from Hong Kong because I felt on edge and trapped in silence. I allowed him to dump his shit, sad energy, on me and I allowed him to steal my joy. It also didn't help that the young man next to me was passing gas throughout the whole flight. His shitty smell killed my nose for hours. I just cried in sadness of the shit that I was in. Mr. Swiss sat next to me and never asked me anything. He ignored my sobbing and the smell of they guy next to me. I was next two men, shitting on me and I could not do anything about it.

For the next two days after our trip to Asia, I continued to cry, and Mr. Swiss didn't ask me anything. He just ignored my sadness.

This drove me crazy! I became his emotional punching bag.

This emotional punching bag was my role, and I played it well. I lost myself in his silence, drama, and anger. I took on all of his emotions and made them mine. The volcano was brewing, and I was getting a piece of its ashes through his words of anger, distrust, and insecurity. I couldn't stand feeling like I was on edge or he was on edge because I was unsure when he was going to have an emotional outburst of blaming.

He would first question my happiness.

"Why do you make it seem like you have a good life?
What successes have you had to share with people when you have only been a mother?
Why do you make people think you are happy on social media?"

He would follow up with a barrage of questions about my business and volunteer work.

"How can you coach a professional, who have you coached before?
You haven't worked in a long time so what job can you get?
Just have a passion don't try to work?

Aren't you happy being a mom?
Who are you networking with?
Why are you doing this internet radio show and who are you talking to?
Why are you doing the blog?
Why are you volunteering at the school?"

There were also questions and statements about his distrust of the people around me.

"Who is this person?
How do you know them?
How long have you known this person?
I don't trust him/her.
Where are you going?
Can I come with you?"

Then, it was the slamming of doors, the shouting matches, and the blaming of everything that he felt was wrong in our world on me. I felt like I was being forced to choose between being an individual or being a trophy wife and super mom. Plus, I remained distrustful of him. It crippled me.

July 2015

July seemed to approach fast. We were off to the Little People Association (LPA) Conference for my daughter, Ivy, to meet friends and to get to know other LP's her age. It was business as usual on this trip, fake smiles, and a busy schedule filled with seminars and group talks. We met awesome people and had a very good time, but there was no love making or physical attention to one another. We were distant.

After the LPA trip, we returned home and, the next day, Mr. Swiss' family came to visit from Switzerland for one month. The first person to arrive was Mr. Swiss' sister-in-law, who came with her son. She wanted a breather because of the unforeseen events a few months earlier. She was unaware that I was looking for the same breath of fresh air. She wanted a month of clarity or at least two weeks until her husband, Mr. Swiss' brother, arrived.

Mr. Swiss' sister-in-law, Mrs. G, and his nephew were super excited about visiting us, and I was excited about having their company. She was actually visiting me because Mr. Swiss was still traveling each week for several days at a time and most of the entertaining fell on me. Because of the language barrier, I knew this would be exhausting. Yet, I also knew that having them in the house was a good distraction from our core problems.

Mrs. G's English was as bad as my German. We understood many words, but it was hard for us to converse fluently. The language barrier didn't stop us from communicating because she talked to me through Google Translate. We also used her son to translate many difficult, lengthy conversations. I realized quickly that she had a lot on her mind, and she wanted to share her thoughts with me without our overseers watching. These intimate conversations were important because we both were in silent cages within our relationships.

She was worried about the two brothers and their lack of emotions towards their parents passing away. I was concerned about the same thing. As we spoke each night, we discussed our husbands' silence regarding their true feelings and how those feelings sometimes came out in anger or retreat. I thought I was in wonderland speaking to her. I was lost in her words because her relationship was my relationship. We shared the fear of their real feelings toward us. We also feared our husbands were leading double lives. Their silence crippled our spirits.

As we talked, I became saddened by her stories regarding the history of his family: the secrets and lies that they kept from the outside world. Their father had another family hidden while his mother suffered emotional and verbal abuse for years. As I listened to the stories of his family's dark secret, my distrust for Mr. Swiss grew even more. Was he lying to me? What was he hiding? Who was he telling his intimate thoughts?

Who is this stranger in my bed after 18 years?

Crippled by her words of her own distrust and fears, I began to believe that I was in a bipolar relationship with a man I didn't really know.

This was some absolutely crazy shit! WDF?!

The Stranger in my House

That summer, we had many visitors, his family, my extended family, and my friends all came to stay at our house. We were running a bed and breakfast for six weeks. At one point, there were fifteen people in our house at the same time. I loved it because it helped me cope with my troubles. It was my distraction and my excuse to avoid Mr. Swiss.

As people kept on visiting, the same questions kept coming up.

What's going on with you guys?
What wrong with Mr. Swiss; he seems to be very distant?
Why does he have to travel so much?
Is he always staring at you?
He seems to be needy?
Why are you so angry?
Timna, why are you whispering?
Timna, you seem to be drinking a lot?
Is Mr. Swiss okay?
Are you okay?
Are you guys okay?

I answered all questions with the same standard lie, *"We are all okay in the this house. Don't worry all will be okay."* Although people saw our pain right through our fake relationship, we continued to hide instead of looking into the mirror.

Distrust - Lies - Secrets - False Happiness - Depression

When his family left to go back to Switzerland, I found myself needing to let my voice be heard. I felt like I was in a golden silent cage with no key to be free. I had to express myself for many to hear, so I started an internet radio show to discuss relationship issues. Starting the radio show did not sit well with Mr. Swiss because he is a very private person.

However, I am not. I needed to start something for myself. I wanted to share my voice. I couldn't be quiet anymore about my thoughts regarding unhealthy versus healthy relationships.

In the fall, we purchased a new home, a large single-family house with four bedrooms, and three baths. We were excited about this new beginning. We decided to renovate our new home before moving in. The renovation brought about a feeling of newness and excitement because we knew that this would be a new start.

However, the excitement of the new house came and went because the clouds keep on hovering over our heads in anticipation of the next storm.

The Sprinkles

It was raining outside, thundering and lightning, the kids were asleep and we were in bed. I was reading some coaching documents and Mr. Swiss was on his computer. He turned to me with fear in his eyes and said, *"Timna, I'm concerned that I bought this home with you."* He continued, *"I'm concerned that by purchasing this home, you will leave me and you will try to take everything."* I was shocked and my heart started to race. I just stared at Mr. Swiss in silence. He was referring to his recent inheritance that he had received from his grandmother and used to purchase our new home.

Excuse me!
What?
I am super confused.
What is he saying?
Why would he think that I was going to leave?
WDF?!

Then, I became angry but remained silent. So I'm not worth him buying a house with me?

Then, my anger became my pain, my fear, my hurt, and I felt emotionally destroyed. He didn't trust the love that I had for him. He didn't trust my intentions for the relationship. Then, he said the most f*cked up thing, *"I* *think you love the relationship more than me."* I shook my head and started to cry. I said quietly, *"What are you saying to me? What are you thinking? Why do you think that I don't love you and just the relationship?"* He said, *"I don't trust you. I don't trust your intentions. It feels strange investing in something that you can't trust."*

I just wanted to punch the shit the out of him! Excuse me! What? I don't understand. This is so messed up!

So, I said, *"I'm going to act like I didn't hear that."* Then, I said, *"I love you! I love this relationship. I will never divorce you. I will never take everything from you. I'm not that person, and I'm sad you think that way about me."*

I cried myself to sleep and tried to forget the conversation because I knew that he was just throwing his words around and he didn't mean what he was saying.

The volcano was brewing knowing that it will soon erupt!

The next day, we acted like that conversation was a dream, that it didn't exist, and that I wasn't hurt from his mistrust. I couldn't breathe around him and he couldn't breathe around me. I waited for him to travel to let my hair down and to build my business. I was relieved when he travelled. I was free of the constant reminder of his distrust. Still, I stressed about his whereabouts, with whom, and where he was having fun. I wondered who he was sharing his thoughts and desires with because it was not me. He also became worried about what I was doing. We started spying on each other. He was spying on me, and I was spying on him.

We moved into a house that apparently symbolized his distrust of me. The cameras that surrounded the exterior of the house made me feel watched. We mistrusted each other; it was strong and apparent. Mr. Swiss would look at his phone and show me that he could see the perimeter of the house wherever he was. This behavior didn't comfort me because I felt like I was being stalked, followed and reviewed. I was insecure about the security that surrounded my home. This security was not for my well-being, but to control me. It felt like Big Brother was watching. He knew when I left the house, when I came in, and what I was doing. He made this clear by calling me as soon as I opened the door after going out to a networking event or calling me as soon as I left the house to find out my schedule for the day. These calls were not calls of concern, but him showing his power of control.

The control made me feel caged. I felt sick and paranoid about Mr. Swiss' intentions. The relationship was coming to a volcanic eruption because I was trapped and needed a way out. Trust was a thing of the past; deception, silence, passive aggression, and a lack of communication were our new reality.

"A Man is not what he thinks he is, he is what he hides."

André Malraux

Chapter 12:
The Problem with Texting

Two things can destroy a relationship: lack of trust and lack of communication.

Even though our situation was a hot mess; I was trying to be sexually attracted to him. I also communicated about the distance and the problem that we silently were going through. At this time most of our conversations were through text.

Texting can help with communication or not!

Me:
I cook, and I make an effort to start working out again. I just hate when my sex drive is high, and I am not fully passionate with you. It's a horrible feeling; I want us to be equal. A lot of women keep things to themselves and gain weight or get depressed. I choose to share my thoughts with you. Even if it's not something you want to hear, I am telling my truth.

Mr. Swiss:
You can always tell me something, but the timing was my issue as I had to leave the house at 6 a.m. to golf, and it was not fun playing golf overtired.

Me:
Again Sorry! The timing was for sure off, but this was the only time that I had your true listening ear. The last time I talked to you, I was so emotional, that I cried for 2 days. This time I was getting clarity with my issue by communicating with you.

Mr. Swiss:
All OK.

Me:
Ok, enjoy. I am going to make the bed.

Mr. Swiss
I know what I need to do and fully agree with you!

Me:
This conversation is the reason I want counseling. My lack of passion towards you is ripping me apart. This is my issue.

Mr. Swiss:
OK

Me:
Passion is through kissing, and a much- needed kiss is important to release passion from someone!

Mr. Swiss
From you partner you mean? That is what I don't like....

Me:
Of course!

Mr. Swiss
Your choice of wording

Me:
When I say, someone, it is a figure of speech. Don't read too hard into it.

Mr. Swiss:
That's how you spoke last night. Just saying... Anyway, I understand.

Me:
The release of passion from yourself and your partner.
We do not kiss, or it's not enjoyable. Hmm... Maybe we should take a Kamasutra class for passionate kissing! That would be awesome! I love you, and I want us to address this problem and solve it!

Mr. Swiss:
Agreed

I knew that we had a continuous problem that was not going away. We were roommates and we had sex. We were not making love and we definitely were not kissing. Not being able to kiss was my issue and I tried to explain this to Mr. Swiss. But he just wanted to get rid of the problem by not truly solving the problem. He just kept on sweeping it under the rug, and I allowed it.

Mr. Swiss' busy schedule left little time for conversation about our problem. When we saw each other, we just continued our lives like the conversation never happened. He agreed that there was a problem, but was silent in person about it. So, we continued Living Life 4 Real in silence.

The Holidays

The holidays came quickly, and all of my immediate family was coming plus a couple of my close cousins.

It was show time!

We were hurting and passive aggressive, but we knew that it was show time. My mom arrived first. After staying for several nights, she stated that she was uncomfortable in my home; I was defensive, but I knew what she was trying to say to me. I ignored it. I was fighting the feeling of discomfort because I was comfortable in my relationship. I was off balance. I tried to stay afloat with each day that passed focusing on my new career endeavors, the girls, and covering up our sadness. This balancing act caused a serious disconnect between my mother and me. I was always super tired and irritable. A couple of weeks later the rest of the family arrived. I tried to be my happy go lucky self, but again, I was pulled in several different directions.

Drained of all positive energy, I decided to go on strike: no cooking and no real hospitality.

The New Year was approaching, and I kicked everyone out! I was done! Baked! I couldn't take it anymore. I needed everyone gone by the first of the year. I wanted to go to a hotel, run away and forget about my worries. I was fighting with everyone not knowing that I was truly in a battle to save my relationship.

The pressure of "til death do us part" was killing me. I unconsciously wanted out of my relationship, but I didn't say it, think it, or acknowledge my true feelings. I just wanted to start the new year refreshed.

The New Year 2016

We started off with a pop of Champagne, a fabulous family dinner, and the relaxation of staying in a luxury hotel. It was a fantasy, and we welcomed it

The New Year and a new relationship. I thought this would be a restart, a refresh of the old, with a look forward to something new. However, it was not new; it was not a restart. It was just an extension of the past.

We needed to make a real change but where should we start? A marriage counselor or a coach? I wanted us to see a counselor to talk about our problems because I was fighting for the relationship. Mr. Swiss didn't see the purpose of going to the counselor because he thought that if we saw a counselor, we would end up divorced. He was scared that a counselor would destroy what we had.

I was confused by this concept. I wanted us to see a counselor because I was tired of this unhealthy relationship and I needed to talk for real about our relationship with a third party. I knew that this was important because I was uncomfortable being in this habitually bipolar relationship. I was tired of the same old story of distrust and a lack of true love.

We were fighting over silly things like who was going to do the girls' hair, which was clearly my job. I now believe this was a manufactured argument because this was something that I clearly loved to do and in my culture, it is a bonding experience between mothers and daughters. We argued about who was going to take out the garbage. He did not want to do this because it was clearly his job. Our roles were a mess. He didn't want to take out the garbage or do any "man's work." He fought me on everything that would secure the house. I felt like I was living with a person that wanted something to happen to the house and his family. He was not protecting his environment. He just looked at me when I cleaned, cooked, or took care of the kids. I felt like a slave in my house. Working with no reward. I was working double time on my new adventure as an internet radio host, blogger, coach, and super mom.

There were no compliments, no acknowledgement of my contribution to the relationship. Mr. Swiss just saw the money that he was bringing home and that this should be enough. The questioning became more frequent:

Why do you need to work?
Why aren't you happy just being with the kids?

Why are you doing so much?
Why do you have the blog?
Why are you on the radio so much?
Why are you volunteering at school?
Why wasn't the house clean when I returned home?
Why didn't you cook?
Why? Why? Why??

There were never any solutions, just a lot of questions. There were no compliments, no concern about whether I liked my new adventure or how I felt. There were only the side comments of a critic.

When you're a stay-at-home parent, you give your partner more control over you. Is he/she using this power to benefit the house or to benefit himself/herself?

Someone asked me this and I had to take a step back. I finally realized that I was being controlled and I was under his spell. My overseer, Mr. Swiss did not want to lose control, so he was stressing me about staying at home so that I would remain dependent on him. I knew that his greatest fear was that I would run away because I would see a light out of this unhealthy bipolar relationship. I had not seen the light yet though.

The Beginning of the End

Time passed by and it seemed that the family was fully booked every weekend. My job each week was to give Mr. Swiss the schedule for the weekend, and he would jump in with some resistance. On this particular weekend, I gave him the schedule and there were some last minute changes, which is often because of the girls and their last minute playdates or activities. So, this particular Saturday, we were supposed to meet as a family and run with other families for a charity event. I told him this, but I was unsure if I was running or just sending the kids with another family. Then, I decided at the last minute to put on sneakers and running pants. He saw how I was dressed and how the kids were dressed but he decided not to wear running shoes.

When we arrived at the event, the girls said they wanted us to run with them. He looked at himself, looked at me and the other people. He became angry. He started to blame me. He shouted, *"Why didn't you tell me to wear sneakers or bring them?"* He began screaming at me in front of people stating that I messed up and that I should have told him about the schedule and that I was not clear. I took one breath and said that I was sorry. I stood there explaining that I was fully engaged with the kids trying to get out of the house and I assumed that he didn't want to participate. I told him that he was a grown man and I couldn't pay attention to him, the new dog, the kids, and myself. He was so irritated that he jumped in his car and peeled out of the parking lot with force.

Another parent looked at me and asked, *"Is everything okay?"* My girls and I said, *"Oh he always gets angry."* I added, *"He has occasional outbursts. He will calm down. He forgot his sneakers and was blaming me. I'm not going to worry about him. I will participate in the run with the girls."*

My own words echoed in my head. This behavior was part of a pattern. He always had outbursts, slammed doors, raised his voice, drove his car off dangerously fast, and blamed me for everything that he felt had gone wrong. I was disgusted with myself and what the girls saw on a normal basis from their dad. I was pissed with myself for acting as if this behavior was okay. It hit me like a brick! This is unacceptable! We needed counseling and now.

He drove back and caught up with us. He didn't speak to me, and I didn't speak to him. I was disgusted by him, and he was still angry with me. We knew that this was the beginning of the end.

Later that day, I received a text from Mr. Swiss stating that we should research counselors. I was super surprised and excited. Finally, we are going to see a counselor. Yippee!

That night, I immediately started to research counselors and gave him a list of qualified marriage counselors. He was surprised at my quick response with names. He just looked at me in astonishment but didn't say anything. Over the next few days, he made excuses when I tried to schedule one of the counselors for an initial session. He also complained that my choice was not right for him. Then, he told me just to book it. Finally, when I called to make some appointments, the counselor was busy the whole week.

Once again, a couple of weeks passed by and we didn't meet with anyone. He was traveling during the week; so there was no way to book an appointment. Mr. Swiss designated the weekends as being for family time. Once again, we swept the problem under the rug and were living life like nothing happened.

The Counselor

Mr. Swiss surprised me when he researched a therapist. I reviewed information on the therapist that he sent me. He was an older White guy, who had worked with families and married couples for over 30 years. Yippee! I was excited that this guy was legit and that we were finally going to see a counselor to help us with our core problems. The day came for us to go to the appointment and he sent me the address. We went together; I had prepared my questions and topics of concern. I was ready.

Then…

While sitting nervously in the waiting room, I noticed there were numerous counselors associated with the office. This office was unusual because it did not have a front desk clerk, just rooms where individual counselors held sessions.

A woman walked out of one of the rooms. She was a tall, Hispanic woman with long curly black hair. She was a bit sexy and provocative. Her tight black pants, boots with 4" heels, and black framed glasses made the office feel very dirty. Is she a sex therapist or the secretary? Mr. Swiss is sexually attracted to this type of woman.

Hmmm… This is strange. Then she reached out her hands and said, *"Hello you must be Mr. and Mrs. …"* Again, I wondered if this was the therapist's secretary.

Then...

We followed her into one of the small offices in the back of the hallway on the right side. There was a gray love-seat, a small desk and a single comfy chair. Along side the chair was a side table. She sat in the single chair near the side table, crossed her long legs and pulled out her pad with a pen and then started to talk. Her accent was thick. She was indeed Hispanic. With her strong Latina accent, she asked, *"So how can I help you guys?"* I looked at Mr. Swiss in astonishment. Why hadn't he told me that he switched the therapist? Who is this woman? What are her qualifications? WDF?!

I lost it inside; my temperature started to rise, I couldn't listen to her, and I couldn't look at him. She looks like a dominatrix! Where am I? WDF?!

Then...

There was a silence, they both looked at me and she asked the question, *"So why are you here?"* Why am I here? Excuse me? But I said, *"Are you our therapist?"* She said, *"Why did you ask this?"* I said, *"I thought you were the secretary of the guy that I had been told we were seeing. I had no idea that my husband changed the therapist. So, I'm sorry if I was taken aback, but if we can start over, with you introducing yourself with your qualifications that would be great."*

She then told us that her specialty is sex therapy, abuse, marriage counseling, and she also works also with the LGBT community.

Okay. I'm confused, but I will go with the flow. Then she wanted to know who would go first to describe our situation. This was, by far, the most interesting and enlightening conversation that I have ever had with another person about my relationship. I realized that my spouse was unaware of our core issue and thought that we needed to spice up our sex life!

Hmmm... No!

Our core issue was the lack of trust! If there is no trust, there is no sex, no intimacy, and no real communication. There is nothing. I told her of his gambling and he told her of my affair. This conversation needed more than an hour. I noticed that Mr. Swiss was so calm, and I was the one getting angry. I felt judged, as if I was being viewed as **"The Angry Black Woman."** So, I told her that my core issue was the loss of trust since the gambling and that it had never been resolved.

He felt that I was not respecting him and that he needed to be able to voice his opinion regarding the kids schedule and the overall management of the home. Isn't that my job?

Time was up!

The session was too quick and I felt like we needed intensive counseling to get to our root problem which was trust. She said that we needed to work on listening to each other more and stop blaming/battling. We needed to stop, think, not start off a conversation using the word no, and to listen to the other partner in order to improve our communication. I left feeling excited about this homework assignment and was ready to start the conversation off without saying, no. I was ready for us to start listening and communicating better. I was also ready to see her again even though she was not who I was expecting at all.

As we started to drive off, Mr. Swiss looked at me with anger in his eyes and said, *"Why would you throw me under the bus? Why would you tell her about my gambling?"* It was the first time I became afraid of Mr. Swiss and thought that he was going to hit me. His anger was so strong; his words were so raw. I felt like a victim. Was I Tina and he Ike? I moved away from him, closer to the passenger door. I felt like jumping out.

Was I driving in the car with the enemy?!
WDF?!

I turned to him with caution and said, *"Aren't we supposed to talk about the past to understand the core issues? Isn't that what counseling is all about?"* Then, he looked at me and said, *"Well if you throw me under the bus again, I will not go back. So next time, don't throw me under the bus. We can talk about communication problems, not my past. If I want to talk about my past, I will."* I sat there in amazement.

Where am I? Who am I? What is going on?

I also asked him about getting a Swiss passport because the therapist had mentioned that her husband had given her one after being married for a few years. He stated, *"You don't deserve a passport."* Wow! Amazing! Nineteen years of marriage and didn't deserve a dual passport.

WDF?!

I told myself, that he was angry and that I should let him cool down. I actually made excuses for his outburst and his anger.

I wanted to return to the counselor, so I decided to tread lightly around Mr. Swiss. I also needed to use the counselor to my strategic advantage. I needed to open up Pandora's Box to seriously understand our problem within our relationship and ourselves. We needed to face what was lingering in the dark, what was hovering over us like a dark cloud waiting to burst.

We started to work on her assignment, which was not to start off each sentence by saying, no. This was difficult because it was a habit. We both noticed that we have begun each sentence of our conversations with the word, no. We quickly noticed that with each spoken word, we were in a battle. Changing this bad habit allowed us to stop, think, and then speak within a discussion. I started to become more aware of my conversations with people and how they received my message.

Even though we were working on communication, I was still hurt by his past words and action. I told my business coach how I felt. I told her that I felt like a battered woman without physical scars. I was so ashamed of myself for moving closer to the passenger door as he shouted at me. I felt defenseless against the anger in his voice. She told me of her story. She was in a verbally abusive marriage which became physically abusive. She divorced him after years of physical abuse. She said that she lost everything and was able to build herself back up. I told her that she was brave and that I was not in that situation. However, I felt like I didn't have the power to leave. I felt weak in my situation because of the money, the glitz, the glam, and the lifestyle that we had built. Plus, where would I run or hide? My parents had moved to Costa Rica.

She asked me, *"How much will it take? What will be the next excuse?"* She also told me that I was in a spiritual battle with my partner, and I needed to look deeper within myself regarding why. Our meeting was powerful. I started to think more about my situation, and I began to cry. I knew that I was trapped and I did not have the will power to say enough is enough. Instead, I was fighting for the relationship, and wanted to work on building it up again.

I went back to the counselor. I was ready to tell her about our disagreement in the car regarding his gambling years. I also wanted to tell her that I was frightened in the car by his aggressive tone and words. Mr. Swiss was traveling, so he missed this appointment, and I used it as individual therapy to recharge. The crazy thing is that, when I called to say that he was not coming, she told me that he canceled the appointment because he would not be there. I told her the meeting was not canceled and that I was coming. I felt like he was controlling even the counselor and the weekly meeting. My trust for his intentions was zero.

I walked into the counselor's office the day of the appointment, and she was all ears. I was ready to share everything that was on my mind. I expressed my distrust, and how I had felt in the car. She told me that I needed to ask him about his truth and to be patient because he could still have resentment about my infidelity. I thought about his resentment about my betrayal. I thought about him and his feeling regarding what I had done. But I also felt like that was years ago and a lot had happened since that time. I wanted him to regain trust in me and I wanted to regain trust in him.

Trust was our core issue.

I left the counseling session knowing that we needed to regain trust. How were we supposed to do this when the trust was broken years ago by both of us? I was ready to do this. Was he? He first needed to see that we had a problem. So, I spoke to him about the session and told him that our core issue was trust. He didn't feel that this was the issue that we faced.

At our next appointment, the therapist asked us how we were doing. We both felt like things were going better. However, we still had different views of what the core issue was. He didn't understand why I stated that I was fighting for the relationship and I didn't understand, why he had the extreme outburst of anger.

He thought that the relationship was fine and that the issue of communication was the key issue. He felt that I was still disrespecting him and not listening to him or having a clear schedule or plan. That's why he had the outbursts towards me, not because of distrust, but a lack of clear communication.

I knew that the relationship was going under and that I was swimming against the tide at all time. I was struggling to keep my sanity, my patience for the relationship, and my ability to keep dealing with his angry outbursts, lack of trust, manipulation, and lack of support for my professional endeavors.

We were each completely in disagreement as to what our core issue was. We needed help. The therapist assisted us with the realization of our disagreement on what our core issue was. We decided to work on both issues at the same time for the rest of that week. We took each problem and dissected the issue and worked towards a common goal each day.

He worked hard each day to be more transparent in his daily travels and his schedule. He put time aside to work on my business and the family goals when he was home. He was making an effort. I even told everyone that the counseling was going great and that we were doing fine.

I made myself less vocal about my feelings, gave him the girls' schedules and allowed him to give input into their lives. I was tip-toeing around him so that I could prove that I was not the cause of his outburst. I also asked him about my business and implemented his advice even if I didn't agree with it. We both were trying our best to rescue the relationship, but the core issue seemed to linger. We met with the therapist the fourth time, and we told her that things were looking up.

May was going by fast and each weekend, we were working on being on our best behavior. We still didn't see each other that much because of Mr. Swiss' crazy travel schedule. We saw each other about seven times that month. Things seemed to be going well.

However, we were still not intimate and I was not my complete self. We were living together tip-toeing around each other.

Our volcano became active again.

Mr. Swiss and I were helping my daughter with her cooking show. I jokingly said, *"You're messing her up and you're in her way. That's why certain parents shouldn't be helping their kids in the kitchen."* I started to laugh. Then, oh my goodness! The camera had to be turned off because he lost his shit in front of the girls.

He started to get angry, feeling that I disrespected him in front of them and that I was belittling him on camera. I told him that he was crazy and I was just joking. However, this didn't sit well with him. He became belligerent and started to yell. He continued to shout that I had disrespected him in front of the girls and stormed out of the house. He yelled, *"I'm leaving!"* The girls were crying, and I felt that all hell had broken loose in just two minutes. After he stormed out of the house, I calmed the girls down. They were crying and asking, *"Where is daddy?"*

I thought everything was okay. What just happened? I am super confused! After the girls calmed down, I told them that daddy had an outburst and he would be back. He just needed to cool down. I told my daughter to continue cooking, and I would film the rest of her cooking show. I embraced my youngest daughter and explained to her that people sometimes cannot control their anger when they feel like they've been embarrassed. I told her that this was not good behavior and that her dad needed to take a walk to calm down. We continued like nothing happened.

He came back huffing and puffing. I ignored him and acted like he was invisible and continued to eat dinner with the girls, cleaned the kitchen, and put them to bed. He wanted to talk to me and I just ignored him. I hid my feeling of disgust. I was fearful of him because he had exploded without reason once again. I was tired of his outbursts, his disrespect, and now his blatant disrespect in front of the girls. This was just unacceptable.

The following week we went back to the counselor, and I told her what happened, and she stated to me that I could've handled the situation differently. She asked, *"What could you have said differently that would have prevented his outburst."* I looked at her puzzled. I felt that she was taking his side. What could I have done differently? Nothing. He could have been a good man, dad, and husband and not disrespected me in front of our girls. He could have controlled himself knowing that we were live on the internet. I asked, *"If he can control himself at work in a high-pressure situation, why can't he control his words and his anger in front of his wife and children? Would he disrespect a person that cursed him out at a meeting? No! I didn't curse him out; I just said two sentences that he didn't like. That's it."*

He stormed out of the therapist's office!

I looked at her and said, *"We are back where we were a couple of months ago."* Later, he came back and we went over the incident again and I took responsibility for my action and he took responsibility for his.

I was a mess after this!

My love for him deteriorated and I felt like I was saying sorry for something that I was not responsible for. I was pissed that I was saying sorry for nothing. That week, I was a mess and I couldn't talk to people. I clearly showed my depression over the relationship. I felt battered, abused, and unheard. I felt like he could say anything, do anything, and no one would understand or feel my pain at his disrespect towards me. I started to tell everyone that our relationship was not good and he was not so nice. I felt like I was in fake relationship. I was fake and he was fake.

We had two more family trips planned for the summer, so I knew that I needed to find my joy and get out of my rut. I hated being that person who brought sadness and drama to a party. I became that woman who was sad in her relationship.

I spoke to a few friends and my business coach who told me to pour myself into my work and my kids. They told me to get refocused and get it together. So, I decided to travel to Florida to have time alone by myself to refocus. I didn't want to see anyone or talk to anyone. I just wanted to sit by the ocean and breathe. Before I left, I saw an intuitive coach to assist me in working through my drama. The crazy thing was when I walked into the room she said, "*Hmmm... I feel the D word.*" I said, "*The D word?*" She said, "*Yes. Are you getting a divorce?*" I said, "*No! What are you talking about? I'm not getting a divorce.*"

I was so angry that she would think that I would think about divorcing my husband. Why would I do such a thing? Then she changed the subject, and we talked about my self-doubt and feelings of being overwhelmed. Then she began to talk about my relationship again, this time about my resentment towards Mr. Swiss. We then talked about my resentment of his financial betrayal towards the family in the beginning of the relationship and my fear of separation. She stated that I needed to love myself and forgive him whether we stay together or not because my resentment would make me sick.

I left our session feeling like I needed to cleanse myself and look deeper into the reason why I was in this relationship and to release the resentment I felt towards him.

A few days later, I walked around my house and knew it was truly time for a change. I felt the need for a change and I told Mr. Swiss about my feelings I needed a change. He once again agreed.

The trip to Florida was amazing, I needed the time for me to build myself back up, both mentally and spiritually. Mr. Swiss spent time with the girls and all seemed well again. He was in his space, and I was in mine. A week later, I returned. Then I was off again to help a friend. We didn't see each other for two weeks.

As soon as I returned, he was on a plane traveling for work. We were passing each other by not changing anything. When we finally saw each other, we were like long lost lovers. We were moving fast and living in a fantasy world.

Colorado

It was time for us to do our spring trip with the girls in April and we chose Colorado. We arrived at the small, cozy condo where our friends lived part-time. The condo was enough space for us to be comfy and cozy without any issues. I thought everything was going well. We got skies for the kids and went shopping. The days were going to be full of skiing, sun and fun.

After a day of skiing with the kids, Mr. Swiss asked me to meet him and the girls for lunch near the mountain. I arrived promptly in a great mood. I was happy to see them and they were excited to see me. We were searching for a restaurant to have a late lunch. I was unsure of where to go and thought that they had already spoken about where they wanted to eat. While walking through the village with the girls, we discussed which restaurants we wanted to dine in. Mr. Swiss decided on an Italian restaurant where he said he had eaten before. I was super relaxed about the idea, but the girls were not that interested. We sat down and were informed that the kitchen was only serving pizza, which Mr. Swiss and one of my daughters didn't want. He then turned to me and started blaming me for picking the restaurant. I was shocked because I didn't have anything to do with the choice of restaurant. So then, both the girls and Mr. Swiss started blaming me for the wait, the limited selection, and the fact that everything was wrong. Something came over me, and I began to cry. This was the first time that the girls had seen me cry and I realized that I was tired of Mr. Swiss blaming me for everything. I couldn't stop crying. The girls asked me what was wrong and Mr. Swiss just looked at me in disbelief. He said, I was hormonal. I was disappointed in him and how he was allowing the girls to speak against me as well. I was in shock over the whole experience.

The next day, I was distant and questioning my situation. What is going on in my world? How did I get here? What is going on?

A couple of days passed and the distance was evident. We had limited conversation. He went skiing all day and the girls were in ski school. I wandered the city keeping busy, entertaining myself.

One morning Mr. Swiss woke up and was even more quiet than normal. I asked him *"Is everything okay?"* He said, *"I was thinking that you think that you are entitled to my money. I think that you feel entitled to this relationship. You think you have it too good."*

I looked at him with amazement, and I was shocked! Entitled? In a calm voice because the kids were next door in the other room, I said, *"I would love for you to look this word up while I take a shower because I want you to be clear on what you're saying to me."*

I jumped into the shower and I was furious! I was boiling up with anger and frustration. I took a long shower to calm myself down because the girls were in the other room and the apartment was small. I didn't want to lose myself and have an argument with this person that I call my husband. I was so done with him and his shit!

ENTITLED?! Are you serious?! ENTITLED?!

I was softly screaming inside the shower and letting the water beat down on me to clear my head with this nonsense that I was hearing from my husband.

Entitled?!

- I'm the mother of your kids.
- I stopped working to raise these kids.
- I opted out of being a career woman.
- I could have been making $150K if I had continued working.
- I could be divorcing your ass, but I chose to be with you.
- These kids, this home would not be what it is without me and the experience I bring to the table.
- You would not be where you are without a supportive, educated wife, coach, trainer, and adventurous lover.

- I moved more than four times for your career advancement.
- My resume is jacked the f*ck up because of you!
- ENTITLED? Are you serious?!
- I deserve everything I have.
- WDF?!

So, I came out of the shower with a relaxed looked on my face, soft voice and then I asked him, *"Did you look up the word, entitled?"*

He started to read the definition from his phone, *"Believing oneself to be inherently deserving of privileges or special treatment."* So, then I looked at him with a straight face and asked, *"So you understand the definition of this word and you are still saying what you're saying about me?"* He then had to nerve to say, *"Yes."*

I immediately lost my shit (in my mind)!

Then I said calmly, *"Do you think that I'm acting like I'm privileged or that I feel like I'm deserving of special treatment?"* He then had the nerves to say, *"Yes."* This F*cked me up! I was lost inside. Screaming!

I wanted to PUNCH the SHIT out of him.

Then, I calmly said, *"So, you think that I'm entitled and not deserving of what?"* He said, *"You feel entitled to my money and you feel like you are owed something from me when you did nothing to contribute to my success. You act like you have a good life on social media and you make people feel like you're deserving of what I have."*
WDF?!

I was so shocked, that I looked at him and told him, *"I'm walking away and acting like I didn't hear what you just said."* So, I walked away, went downstairs to the small loft condo to start making breakfast for the girls, and acted like I did not have this conversation with him. How can he disrespect me like this? How could he treat me like shit? We just had sex the night before. WDF?! I was f*cked up emotionally, spiritually and I knew I was sleeping with the enemy! He was a stranger; he didn't love me and he didn't care about me. He wanted to break me down slowly. This was too much.

What would I do? Where would I go? Who am I? What is this? Do I even love myself because I have been putting up with this bullshit?

Then, the owner of the house came with her family and of course, we acted like nothing happened and we were friends once again. This show lasted for several days until it was time for us to return to Atlanta.

The day before our flight back home we stayed one night in a hotel nearby the Denver airport. Our room was on the 24th floor, where there was a pool for the girls to swim in and a workout facility.

I thought that everything was back to normal. But once again, Mr. Swiss was angry, distant, and moody. I tried to make peace with him because I hated the negative energy that he was giving me. I wanted him to relax and not be in fear of me leaving and taking everything. After the kids went swimming, hey accompanied Mr. Swiss to the room. I decided to leave them and go downstairs to get him a cocktail and his favorite dessert to make amends for our situation.

I knew he was traveling to NYC the next day, and we wouldn't see each other for another week. I was hurt, but I didn't want us to depart fighting. I came upstairs with his surprise dessert and cocktail. He looked at me with disgust and didn't say thank you or anything. He was silent. This silence killed me. I tried to make him laugh so that the kids could see us happy, but he kept a straight face. We were in a war of silence.

As we laid in the bed together with our laptops opened. It was around one a.m. and a bird hit our window. I looked at Mr. Swiss and he didn't flinch. Then 30 minutes later, another bird flew into the window, this time with a big bang. Again he didn't flinch. I was so agitated and stressed because I knew what the symbol of a bird flying into your window meant. It meant death or a rebirth. I looked over at him and at this point, he was on his phone, huddled and hiding what he was watching, reading or searching. I was disappointed in his lack of reaction or concern of these birds flying into our window on the 24th floor. I closed my laptop, used the restroom, acted like he was not there, and went to sleep.

The next day, he woke up "bright eyed and bushy tailed" ready for the day. He acted like nothing was wrong. Hmmm…. He didn't ignore me. He wasn't rude like the night before. Hmmm... Am I going crazy because he is getting ready like nothing was wrong with us and our communication? He was ready for the day. He looked refreshed, well rested, and was looking forward to catching his flight. I, on the other hand, was tired, frustrated, and emotionally beaten.

We drove to the airport in silence knowing that we would be separating and going to two different terminals. He was heading to NYC, and I was heading back to Atlanta. When we arrived, the girls gave him a hug and he tried to give me a kiss to say goodbye. I was so confused by this kiss. I was taken aback and wondering what was going on. The kiss was horrible, uncomfortable, and disrespectful. I didn't want it, care for it, or need it. I just wanted him gone!

I was hurt, and I told all of my friends that he said that I felt entitled. A dear friend asked me, *"What is your vision of your relationship? When will enough be enough for the both of you guys because you guys clearly have no trust for each other?"* I thought about what my friend said, and I had no answer. I was ashamed of who I was and what this relationship had become, but once again, I swept it under the rug and went about my life with the girls while he traveled. I was happy when he was gone and on edge when he was around.

Two weeks went by where we spoke only briefly via text and had some phone calls regarding the girls. I only saw him on the weekends and they were busy. There was no time to communicate about past issues. Our days and nights went by fast.

The Private Investigator

It was May, a week before Mother's Day. Mr. Swiss was traveling and I received a delivery of flowers. The flowers were beautiful, but I was not happy about the flowers because I thought that the flowers were sent to me out of guilt and not out of love. What is he hiding? What is he feeling guilty about? While thinking these far from happy thoughts, I took a picture of the flowers and posted it with the tagline, "What a great surprise!" Yes, it was a surprise indeed. But was it the surprise that I wanted? What were the intentions behind this surprise?

I called Mr. Swiss and thanked him for the flowers, still wondering why he would send them a week before Mother's Day. So I asked him. He said, *"Everyone sends flowers on Mother's Day. You're not my mother, so I sent them to you today."* Really? I did not believe a word he had just spoken. I was offended, upset, and filled with anger. I knew he was guilty of something, but I couldn't prove it; hence, the flowers. That day after I posted the picture of those beautiful red roses for the world, I opened my computer and started to search for a private investigator in my area. As I researched private investigators, many questions began to flood my mind.

What if?
What if I start to cry?
What would he tell me?
What is his secret?
How much will this cost?
Will this help me to find peace within my dreams?
What would I say or do if I something was revealed to me?
What will happen?
What if there is nothing and I am just going crazy? What if?

I found an investigator, and I called him. The phone started to ring. I was super nervous: my armpits began to sweat, my blood pressure began to rise. I was so nervous. The phone stopped ringing and then, there was a hello on the other end.

PI: *"Hello? How can I be of assistance?"*
Me: *"Oh, my name is Timna. Oh, do you want to know my name?"*
PI: *"How can I help you? Do you want to investigate a cheating spouse or an insurance fraud?"*
Me: *"I am calling to inquire about a cheating spouse. How does this all work?"*

He read me his credentials and told me that usually people already know that something is wrong if they have called him. He asked me whether I wanted his findings to be videotaped, recorded, or just documented. He also asked me if I wanted him to put a trace on Mr. Swiss' car or phone. I immediately freaked out and said, "Wait! This is overwhelming! He travels a lot and so I'm unsure how this will all work."

He said in a sarcastic voice, *"Ahh, that's a different situation altogether and much more money."* I then said, "So, what does a traveling spouse being investigated cost and how does this work?" He started to laugh and asked, *"Well, how much money are you willing to spend?"* I was starting to relax and fired back, "Seriously, how much would this cost me?" *"Well, it depends on where he is traveling and which state because you will need to hire an investigator in each state because licensure in each state is different. I would work with each person to get information about his whereabouts."*

This is too crazy. What the hell am I doing? This is some crazy shit!

I came to my senses and started to laugh with the investigator about my fears of mistrust and cheating. We both decided that it was truly impossible to find out what Mr. Swiss was doing because of his travel schedule. The investigator told me to chill and relax. He said, *"If there is something, it will come to light sooner than later because it always does."*

I knew he was right and that it would all come out sooner or later. However, the waiting game was killing me. The thought of Mr. Swiss hiding something from me grew stronger and stronger each day. I was a hot mess.

Then it happened. The volcanic erupted!

"Over every mountain there is a path, although it may not be seen from the valley."

Theodore Roethke

Chapter 13:
The Volcano

The truth lies inside of your gut.

We went on our last family trip that summer, and the volcanic eruption happened.

It was hot. It was steamy. It was deadly.

The eruption came upon us as soon as we walked into the vacation rental house in San Francisco. It was late, and the darkness was creeping up on us. Vines, bushes, and flower beds covered the entryway of the French style cottage. We opened the door, and as we entered, my daughter, Anavi, and I noticed the paintings on the walls. They were pitch black. Maybe the artist wanted us to use our imagination, but why are these paintings in someone's home? Strange. Then, we walked further into the home. We saw a grand piano, and we could see the backyard where there was a meditation garden. The meditation garden was equipped with small candles, a large peaceful fountain, and a wooden bench. To the left of the grand piano were steps heading to the second floor. Along the side of the steps, there was a small kitchen and there was a giant Buddha that sat snuggled in the corner of a small library.

The house seemed to be closing in on me as I walked through it. I felt like the house was draining my energy and soul. I expressed my discomfort to Mr. Swiss, and he stated, *"I don't feel anything. You're imagining things."* My daughter Anavi seemed to be spooked as well. She started to cry as she walked upstairs with her sister, Ivy. She cried, *"Mommy, I'm scared. This house is scaring me!"* I ran up the stairs to her to console her and noticed a large floor length mirror in the guest bedroom, which was off of the master suite. The mirror was creepy, and it faced directly in front of the bed. There were more black, dark blue, and dark green paintings in the guest room. I agreed with my daughter that the house was a bit spooky and told her that I would talk to Mr. Swiss.

While my youngest daughter and I were feeling spooked, Mr. Swiss and my oldest daughter seemed to be fine. They thought the house was cool not spooky.

I calmed Anavi, then quietly approached Mr. Swiss and told him that if both Anavi and I still felt this way by tomorrow, we would have to get another place to stay. He thought that I was crazy and said out loud, "*Well Ivy and I love it! It reminds me of my mother's house, and you saw it online with me. So, why are you making a big thing about it now! Plus, you're making Anavi feel this way.*"

Once again, he is blaming me in front of the girls and dismissing my concerns. I felt like he was not protecting me, but putting me in harm's way. I wondered why he was so combative over something that was clearly troubling to both his daughter and me.

That night…

That night, I decided to cover the mirror with a blanket, turn on some lights to make the environment less spooky, and I slept with the girls to give them comfort. The next morning, we woke up and Mr. Swiss left early to go to work. We were in a vacation home, but it was only a vacation for myself and the girls. I knew Mr. Swiss had a full schedule, so that morning I planned the rest of the week for myself and the girls. I got to know the house much better. I played music and made it more inviting for the children, but I still felt uneasy.

The girls and I traveled to a gym an hour away from the rental house. Anavi needed to practice gymnastics for a few hours each day to keep up her strength and flexibility. While I was there patiently waiting, I received a text from Mr. Swiss that he was going to stay in a hotel overnight because the company accidentally booked him a hotel stay. For some reason, I immediately lost it! I got angry! I was furious that he was telling me he was going to stay out that night when we had just arrived at a vacation home. A vacation home which most of his family thought was spooky and uncomfortable.

I lost it!
This relationship is bipolar.

The Texts

7/18/16, 8:34 PM

Mr. Swiss:
Shoot... They booked me the room, but I never saw the confirmation... I might stay here as my schedule starts early. Might swing home late to get clothes...

Me:
Whatever.. Who are you staying with and f*cking... Just saying #really! Are you kidding me? I told you ... you're acting weird. You said I want to see the hotel I'm staying at twice today and you also said the word "hotel" several times... You're making me wonder. Dude, are you serious right now?

Me (A few minutes later):
Actually I take this back.... I trust you... Stay overnight at a hotel 5 minutes from our vacation house!

Mr. Swiss:
You can join me... I have no f*cking issue!!! I had no clue! I didn't know.

Me:
Go right ahead I'm giving you permission!!

Mr. Swiss:
F*ck it... You make no sense!!!

Mr. Swiss (a few minutes later):
I will come home... I am in the car right now full of people... Call you when I am there.

Me:
Just saying that was super weird... So I reacting in a way in which you are placing me. But I'm calm now!

Mr. Swiss:
If you trust, then you don't react... So wrong

Me:
I've decided to breathe.

Me (a bit later):
Plus, No, I don't trust you, not when something is last minute and convenient for you. Just saying.....

Mr. Swiss:
They booked two nights but I made them cancel the second night. The confirmation went into my junk. It was my fault as I assumed they didn't book it.

Mr. Swiss: (later)
Whatever on your comment!!!

Me:
Ok.. No problem

Mr. Swiss:
I don't need shit from you! I'm in high pressure meetings and I try to navigate. You should be supportive. I try to fit everything in.

Me:
Excuse me! Thomas really! Check yourself! Understand why I reacted in the way I did and what you did. Don't blame my reaction on me.

Me: (later)
The reaction was because of the cause and effect of the message sent.

Mr. Swiss:
You there?

Me:
One moment.. Talking

Mr. Swiss:
See you tonight...

Mr. Swiss: (later)
I am now going to the cocktail hour...

Me:

You know what's so funny. You would say "not cool!" to your own request. Put yourself in my shoes. I'm super disappointed with you for even considering staying out tonight. It makes me wonder what type of trouble were you trying to get into tonight. #Justsaying! I have trust issues, and you're not helping it.

Mr. Swiss:
I get it. I tried to make the best of what was my mistake. I completely missed an email and that is why I have now a booked room. I managed to cancel the second night without a charge. I will come home and leave early tomorrow.

Mr. Swiss (later):
I now know what I did wrong. I failed to tell you how big of a meeting this is and how important is was to me.

Mr. Swiss (even later):

Mr. Swiss (much later):
You guys ok?

At this point, I was not having it. Even though I tried to calm the situation down via text; I was upset about his disrespect of telling me he was going to stay the night at a hotel. I didn't accept his late night text or hearts. I was emotionally done. I didn't want to be manipulated any longer because I knew he wanted me to crawl back into his web of sweet nothings. The next day, he challenged me on my whereabouts with the girls and his lack of access to me because I wasn't answering his calls or texts. His badgering stressed me out so much.

Two days later, I felt emotionally tapped out, but my actions were different regarding sex. I fell back in the web of trying to fix our problem and coach my way through our relationship issues.

Me:
Good morning.

I just want you to know that I'm still not with the events of Monday and yesterday (challenging me) I think you sometimes have no empathy towards me. You have yet to truly apologize to me. And you enter the house Monday night and startled me. Once again, you disrespect me without texting me to inform me that you were coming home. I do not have to explain myself over and over again about my issues with entering the house. At this point, I feel like you don't care. Which is very sad. I love you, but I think you simply don't give a damn, which is always our main issue (empathy)...(consideration)...

Have a great day and see you later.

P.S. I thought about it having sex once a week is not ok. If I accidentally fall asleep you need to wake me up. I'm not good in the morning, which you are aware. It's been 20 yrs.

Me (later):
I was ready on Sunday night, Monday no because of earlier and last night we could of had sex. Just saying...

Me (Much Later):
Are you not interested?

Mr. Swiss:
I would love to have intercourse with you, but you simply don't get it

Me:
Really???

Mr. Swiss:
Just hear me out and try not to be condescending

Mr. Swiss:
It takes two people. You are mad but you don't talk. You don't give me a heads up about your schedule. You never told me about when you were going to the movie and that you would be an hour late. You set the expectation to pick me up at 6pm then you show up at 7pm without a text.

And FYI; I told the girls that I would come home that night 15 minutes prior to arrival. I assumed that they told you but they fell asleep... No respect? Really... There are two sides to the story. You are mad but don't consider that I am stressed and you don't ask me. You assume I don't care vs give me time.

We have yet had the time to talk! I work and you relax.

Me:
Excuse me! Are you serious? I'm in NO way relaxing!

Mr. Swiss:

Look at your text. It's a reaction to the cause. And again! You text me instead of calling me!

Me:
Stop doing the blame game and you started the texting stuff. How easy did we forget about the events of Monday through text???? #Really
Thomas F*ck you!
Bye

Mr. Swiss.
Thank you for that!

Me:
Bye Thomas. You can be such a Dick! WOW

Mr. Swiss:
I am the dick? Look at it

Me:
Bye Thomas. Go to work because I need time to RELAX!

Mr. Swiss:
And the Monday text? You're mad about something that was never my intention!!!

Me:
Instead of seeing it through my eyes. You continue to attack and bully me. I will not allow you to do this. You bullied me with your first text. Wow.

Mr. Swiss:
That was a text of concern and request

Me:
You don't even see.
This makes me even sadder.

Mr. Swiss:
I didn't think I needed to apologize for anything. You explode at me when I am stressed at a meeting I'm having in a bit!

Me:
Thomas I'm done. No need to apologize. You're always right! You're always on the giving side and you're always the one not starting the argument.

Mr. Swiss:
A simple good morning call would be great!

Me:
You're seriously only thinking of yourself. Please have a great day at work.

Mr. Swiss:
I am not saying that I was right on Monday. But this morning and yesterday evening was uncool. I am sorry you feel this way and I will make it a focus. I was exhausted last night and you throw 20 years at me.

Me:
The kids are up and I need to start my job. Thomas we will talk offline later.

Mr. Swiss:
That is so ridiculous!!! You throw lines at me then say F*ck you. Then say I am done talking. Really?

Me:
It makes no sense to continue texting. The kids are up now and I have to stop texting. My job has started!

Mr. Swiss:
Here is my situation; I woke up at 6 a.m. Prepared for an hour for a meeting that I am trying to turn positive. Then I am getting dressed and heading to the office. I know already that I don't have all the data for the meeting as engineering needs to build it. This restaurant group will be pissed and potentially cancel. The first words I get was how bad I am towards you. Sorry that I react but once I am through this meeting at 10am I will feel a lot better. However, you just added negativity on top of the situation.

Me:
Stop. I can't even read this....

Mr. Swiss:
This meeting makes my stomach turn and I don't even want to go in. That's why I am stressed.

Me:
Bye. We can talk later

Mr. Swiss:
You stop when it's convenient. Read the last string as it gives insight to my stress.

Me:
Ok give me a minute... Kids are talking to me.

Me:
Actually, Sorry, I can't talk right now.

Mr. Swiss:
I am sorry for saying I am working, and you can relax. I know it's not like you have an option. I am appreciative of what you do for the kids and take one for the team. I was reactive as I am truly stressed. I want to hang out but don't have the option... And you then are challenging me by communicating. I will be taking off most of tomorrow and Friday. Today I have several meeting as it is my first full day at the office.Mr. Swiss:
Will call you after my meeting

Me:
I'm just now sitting down to read the previous text.

Me (later):
In response to your text, I'm not challenging you at your job. You don't need to take time off. This is your place of business. The kids and I just fine and I DO understand your day to day stress. That's NOT the issue.

The issues was the lack of empathy towards me and which I have towards you. I don't demand or expect you to go above and beyond, but I expect you to respect me and the things that I do for this team. I don't like to be dismissed or made a fool. Just saying..

Me (later):
I think we both have the same issue and it comes down to unclear expectations. I don't want to fight you on this.

Mr. Swiss:
Anyway, we both ask for the same, which means we're both doing the wrong thing...
Let's have a minute to regroup on this.

We decided not to text each other for the rest of the day to regroup. I spent the day with the girls, and I wanted to forget my negative feelings towards Mr. Swiss. I called several of my friends to talk me off my emotional ledge, and one of my friends asked me a deep question. My guy friend said, *"How long are you going to keep this up? What are you afraid of?"*

What was I afraid of? What was my naked truth? Why was I avoiding my true feelings for Mr. Swiss and my need to leave this relationship?

FEAR

I couldn't answer these questions because I was afraid. Over the years, I learned to stifle my real emotions because I feared the loss of the relationship and my lifestyle. I pondered what would happen if I told him that I didn't want to be with him. What would happen to the girls? I wondered if I could truly love him and if we could have a roommate type of relationship with benefits.

The fear was crippling me all day because I didn't want to talk to him about my true feelings. I thought about my family, his family, our friends, my social community, his social community, his job and how they would feel if I didn't love him. I wouldn't have any money, no lifestyle, no house, and no job. Plus, I helped build him up to be this powerful, successful guy. Do I want someone else to be with him? No. I certainly didn't want that now that he has the perfect smile, perfect job, and has changed his body to be more athletic.

I was scared of the naked truth.

Then it happened that night.

I couldn't sleep, tossing and turning in the bed. My body was cold; I was anxious and I couldn't relax. Why am I afraid? What were my true feelings for Mr. Swiss? It was 12:55 a.m. and I decided to see if any of my friends were still up. I needed a lifeline. I needed to reach out to someone, but no one was available. I then looked over at Mr. Swiss, and I noticed that he was in a peaceful deep sleep. I marveled that he could be so relaxed while I was tossing and turning in the bed. I eventually fell back to sleep. Suddenly, a bright light shined directly into my eyes. I immediately woke up! I looked up at the moon; it was so full and so bright. I couldn't believe that I had only been asleep for 90 minutes. It felt like an eternity. I noticed that I wasn't tired, I was just aware. I looked at my phone and the time was 2:22.

What does this all mean? What does God want to tell me? I decided to walk downstairs to sit near the big Buddha to meditate and be in silence.

There it was, my unspoken realization. I cried. I became weak. I became sick. I cried even more. My path was written, now it was up to me to listen, follow my intuition. I knew it would be painful and unpleasant. I didn't love him anymore; I didn't want to be with him, and I my heart was broken! I continued to cry and mourn the loss of my relationship in this quiet place. I knew that I didn't want to be in the relationship, but I had no plan or way to get out. So, I decided to wipe my tears and head back upstairs because I was trapped. I accepted my fate in my relationship. I told myself, I can do this for several more years until the girls grow up. I can do this for five more years. I told myself that this is all I need.

However, I started to cry again, knowing that I was unhappy in my life. I felt stifled and restricted. I wasn't free to be myself. I was afraid of being alone and not having enough power to be strong for myself and my girls. I laid back in the bed with no way to release my tension. I just laid there crying, paralyzed by my thoughts. My body was limp and broken; I was in my cage. I laid next to the man that captured me. As I continued to lay there with the moon shining on my face, I thought to myself with a pillow case drenched in tears; I have no way out.

The tears ran down my face. There was no sound, just sadness and more tears. I was weak. Then I felt movement and Mr. Swiss woke up with force. He sat up and said to me in a strong voice, *"What's wrong with you?"* I stayed silent. I just wiped the tears from my eyes and stared into to the moon wishing that our volcano would not erupt but I knew it was about to. Then he said, *"What's wrong with you? Do you want a divorce?"* My tears immediately stopped, and my body went into shock! *"Excuse me. What did you say?"* He repeated, *"Do you want a divorce?"* A divorce? Why would he ask me that? I don't want a divorce. I have never wanted a divorce! Then he said, *"It seems like you want a divorce."*

At that point, I found my SHE-POWER. I said in a stern voice, *"You know what? I'm thinking about it because you don't know me! I would never think about divorcing you!"*

I started to question myself and my response. Why would he ask me this crazy question? The volcano erupted. Do you want a divorce? Those words killed my soul, pierced me like a knife. I was stabbed, but no blood was coming out. I felt soaked in invisible blood. I told him that I would never divorce him, but I said, *"I want a separation."*

We laid there in silence. This was a revelation for the both of us! We both questioned the relationship in silence. After, twenty years is it over? My stomach muscles continued to cramp, and my blood pressure started rising. I became dizzy and felt faint. Did I just say what I said? He started to cry as we laid there together on the bed in silence. He cried the ugly cry. He said he couldn't go to work. He couldn't breathe. He couldn't think. All he wanted to do was prevent the inevitable from happening.

We started to talk. He apologized for not listening to me about the weirdness of the house. He had noticed the paintings but refused to acknowledge my concerns. He cried and apologize for unnecessarily battling with me. I laid there with tears in my eyes. I was tired. I wanted a separation and I told him what I needed.

CHANGE! CHANGE! CHANGE!

Then the sun came out, the girls were getting up, and it was time to celebrate my daughter's birthday. It was time to perform in our fake relationship for the girls. It was show time.

My phone rang. It was my dear friend. She called me to see what was going on NOW in my relationship. I walked out on the rooftop patio and began talking to her. Mr. Swiss was stressed because I was on the phone and he needed to perform in front of the girls solo. I had no more tears. I was just angry that he didn't respect me. I felt everything finally came to a head. I was numb with anger. I was ready to make a move.

While was on the phone with my friend she asked me, *"Why do you complain about the same thing over and over again. You've been complaining about his behavior for years, the secrecy, the lies, the mistrust, the stalking, the lack of acknowl-*

edgment, the anger, and the verbal disrespect. When will this complaining stop? When will you say enough is enough? When will you leave?" She told me that she would listen, but it was the same story over and over again. It was a broken record that had been playing for years. I felt bad, and I told her that this time, I would surely do something. She said, *"How do you know that something will change?"* I replied, *"I'm not scared anymore! I'm done! I will now tell him my truth. I don't want to be with him anymore, and I'm leaving!"* She questioned, *"How do you know that you will have the courage to do this?"* I answered, *"This is the first time that I ever said that I want a divorce to anyone. So I'm serious!"* She said with uncertainty in her voice, *"Okay."*

While we were on the phone, Mr. Swiss kept on texting me and calling me. He didn't want to be around the girls because he couldn't control his tears. He was having a breakdown. He thought that if he could manipulate me with his words and tears that everything would be fine. But it wasn't. I was done!

He left to go to work, and he was a mess. He was crying and crying. He kept on calling me and texting me that he couldn't live without me. He told me that he couldn't breathe that he would be nothing without me. He wouldn't be able to live without me. As he pleaded, my compassion for him lessened. My emotions were done, and I became deaf to his words.

In anger, I texted him *"Don't kill yourself because life insurance doesn't cover suicide."* I was so pissed with him that I couldn't feel his cries, his pain, or his words of forgiveness. It all meant nothing to me. I was numb.

Then later on that day, he saw that I was numb, so he tried another tactic to win my heart back. He tried a scare tactic. He texted me that he would sell the house and take the girls. He told me that I wouldn't have any money. He texted me that I would be nothing without him. He texted that I would have to answer to my friends and my family regarding why we were breaking up.

Yes, his scare tactics made me stressed and put me under pressure. However, I found the strength to tell him that I was tired of him dangling the carrot stick and I would be fine with nothing. Yet, in the back of my mind, I was still scared of the loss of my lifestyle.

He came home that night. Despite our continuous angry texts, we went to dinner as a family. We decided to eat at a local Italian restaurant; I walked in first with one of my daughters, and the restaurant owner was noticeably disrespecting me. Even though the restaurant was 40% full, she sat us at the back of the restaurant by the kitchen. I realized that she did this to avoid people seeing us in their restaurant because we were a family of color. The disrespect of her staff and the owner were blatant. I decided to stay because the kids were hungry. Mr. Swiss saw the blatant disrespect but did nothing to help to resolve the situation.

Later that night, he cried and said sorry for disrespecting me and not standing up for me in many past cases of racism, prejudice, and sexism. He started to understand my frustration. He also apologized for competing with me and not acknowledging my role within the relationship.

We also had a conversation about my likes and dislikes. He admitted to deliberately not wanting to acknowledge my likes and dislikes. He acknowledged his relentless avoidance of taking out the garbage or helping me to tidy the house. He confessed to being Silent knowing that it was tearing me apart.

We talked and talked.

I fell back into his web because I felt sorry for him. That night, I fell back into my role of being a wife and submitting to my husband. He was so sweet. He was apologizing and it seemed heartfelt. We even had sex! It felt good, but it also felt so wrong. I felt sick to my stomach. We had sex and I knew he thought this was a sign that everything was okay. He even proclaimed, *"My wife is back."* This statement made me cringe.

Your wife is back? So who is Timna?

As I laid on the bed, he leaned over to give me a kiss on my forehead. The kiss made me feel cheap and sick. I knew he thought everything was okay.

But, it wasn't. I felt like SHIT. I wanted to wash and clean him from the inside of me. As he walked away, I wanted to scream.

I heard his footsteps go down the stairs; I laid there until the front door slammed shut. I immediately got up to wash him off of me. As I approached the bathroom sink, I noticed a note, "Good morning my love." I read it and tears came to my eyes. Who am I? What have I become? He left me a note!

Who is this woman having sex, then being left on the bed while the man gets dressed, kisses his wife on the forehead then goes to work? Am I a slave to this relationship? Am I a prisoner?

WDF?!

Am I being emotionally abused? I gave him sex for payment of me being upset with him.

I needed to WAKE THE F*ck UP!

I got so mad that I ripped the note up and took a shower. I got sick to my stomach. I felt cheap. Who have I become?

So then I started my job with the girls and he sent me a text.

Mr. Swiss:
Are you ok?

Me:
No, I'm busy with the kids

Me (later):
I didn't like the note that you left me. I'm still upset with you. I'm emotionally messed up and I'm uncomfortable with you leaving me a note when I'm still mad with you.

Mr. Swiss:
I'm sorry, maybe I did that too fast. Yesterday, I was wondering where is my wife.

Me:

Where is your wife? Well, stop asking where is your wife and start asking where did Timna go and understand that she is back. Timna is a person, an individual and also your wife. I don't want to do this anymore. Oh, just because we had sex doesn't mean that we're in good standing. I'm done. I think I want a separation from you.

Mr. Swiss:
You want a separation! What does that look like? Where will I go? Do you want me out of the house? For how long? Where is my wife? Who is this person?

The texts continued and both of us were battling for control of the situation. He wanted to understand why I would want a separation and what a separation would do to the relationship. He worried that a separation would eventually lead to a divorce, which he did not want.

In the day, we texted back and forth all day. In the night, we stayed up crying and talking about the past, present, and future. Over the next several days, we talked about our feelings. I became sicker and sicker. My stomach was hurting so much that I couldn't eat and I couldn't sleep. I definitely did not want to be around him. However, he kept pulling me back in, or really, I kept allowing him to enter my mind and plant seeds inside my brain to grow. I was allowing him to manipulate my feelings. I was lost in my emotions. I didn't know what to do and how to say no to his cries for forgiveness. I kept on slipping back into my role of wife and it was killing me inside. My soul was bruised. I felt like an emotionally battered woman. I was lost and I didn't know how to escape.

**I felt enslaved in this relationship, in this love affair.
I wanted OUT. The control had to stop!**

We returned home from our vacation in San Francisco. I approached the door, and the knob felt warm. I opened the door, and the house was burning up hot. It was 116 degrees Fahrenheit! The fireplace was blaring (accidentally left on by one of us) and the house was melting. It was a symbol. Our life was on fire! There was a volcanic eruption in our world and our home represented this.

I looked at Mr. Swiss and he looked at me. We knew that we were in the volcano and we were about to get burned. The representative from the fireplace company told us that if we were away for a few more days the house would have caught on fire. WDF?!

We almost lost everything.

But we did! We lost each other and needed a major change; we needed a restart. We needed to be separated to find ourselves in this relationship that had become an unhealthy habit. Change needed to happen. This was not us anymore. Change became the priority in this unhealthy relationship. We both spent that week on an emotional roller coaster.

Fear
Doubt
Guilt
Anger
Passion
Love
Anxiety

It all came out. One of us needed to leave.

What would the change be?
US

Chapter 14:
4 weeks of Clarity
Change is inevitable

The Separation was needed. It was evident that we disliked each other. We were in a fake relationship. We both acted like someone else to satisfy the pride and desire to be a happily married couple. We had lost ourselves and become strangers. We were both angry on the inside and passive aggressive on the outside. It showed in our kisses or the lack thereof.

We WOKE the F*ck UP and understood the naked truth. That's all! Everyone around us was forced to do the same.

Does he leave or do I leave? The Separation was needed, and it was clear. Twenty years of togetherness, and we disliked each other. Each of us wanted to change the other person. We were angry inside and passive aggressive on the outside. It showed in our kiss (or the lack thereof). Four weeks of clarity would be our silent gift to ourselves and this relationship. It was hard, but it needed to happen. No glitz. No glam. Just self.

I decided that I was going to move. I needed to find clarity and Mr. Swiss did too. We agreed that I would be the one to change my location. I decided to live in Chicago for four weeks. We took two days to discuss what we were about to do. We wanted a "healing separation," where both parties are completely involved in seeking healing of themselves outside of the relationship. We hoped that this separation was to find ourselves; redefine our roles; acknowledge, and accept the resentment that each of us had for the other. We had no idea what the outcome would be, but it was time to find clarity.

I once received a reading from an intuitive woman. She told me that I was going to change my location. She told me this day would happen, but I didn't believe it. He hadn't believed it either.

It happened quickly; my ticket booked and the apartment rented. It was definitely scary, definitely painful, definitely out of character, and it was our awakening.

We had to WAKE the F*ck UP!

That's all!

And everyone around us was forced to do the same.

The Departure

I said goodbye to what I knew was my old reality. I knew the girls would be fine. We had the conversation with the girls and Ivy said, *"Many of my friend's parents divorced and we will be all right. Do what is best for you mommy."* Anavi was just worried about her schedule and her hair. *"Can Daddy take care of us? Can he do our hair? What about school? What about our activities?"*

I made sure to take care of everything before departing. I scheduled the appointments, made a detailed program, and prepared the girls for their new adventure with their Mr. Mom. I knew he could do it, but I also was worried about releasing my control.

He has never been Mr. Mom He doesn't know how to organize the laundry, pack the dishwasher the way I do, cook, clean, do their hair, prepare their clothes for school, wash clothes, and fold the laundry. He didn't know how to prioritize the birthday parties, playdates, bring laughter, confidence, and be an amazing Dad. But I had to find some trust that it would all work out and he would rise to the occasion.

I walked outside of my home to the waiting cab. Mr. Swiss, now Mr. Mom, placed my bag in the car and we looked at each other. Was I supposed to give him a kiss, a hug, a handshake? What should I do? I believe he was wondering the same thing. It was an awkward moment. We looked at each other with sorrowful eyes and we knew it was time to release what we had. It was time to say goodbye without words. I jumped into the car and said bye as he walked away. The girls ran up and gave me a hug. It was time for me to go. It was the longest drive ever. I knew it was time for me to be in silence to reflect and to grow. I had no idea what this would mean to my family and me.

It was the start of my four weeks of Clarity.

Week 1 – Getting Settled

I arrived in Chicago, and my friend greeted me at the airport. She was ready for me to have the best four weeks of my life and to be free from the drama and struggles of my relationship to find clarity for myself. I stayed with her for three days. The first two nights, we partied and had great food, spent several hours at a rooftop party. The partying didn't bring me the joy I had thought it would. It also didn't bring me the freedom that I required. I was still anxious because my friend had her own rules, which made me feel like I was still being watched and under control. I realized that being with a friend was not the same as being alone to find clarity. Even though she was an excellent roommate, I still felt that my days and nights were dependent on someone else. I was not alone with my thoughts.

On day three, I moved to the apartment that Mr. Swiss and I had rented. I was ready to be alone by myself in my silence. I was sad. Moving to Chicago was the realization that my relationship was over. When I walked into the corporate apartment building, I received the keys from the security person and went upstairs while my friend waited for me in the lobby. I stepped into the elevator. Wow, 50 floors; this is huge! Maybe some great people live in this building?

I opened the door to the newly furnished apartment, and I saw the table: it wasn't new, it was weathered; it felt like a college apartment. The furniture was used and dilapidated. I looked outside of this high rise and felt like the buildings were closing in on me. My phone didn't have a cellular connection; this concerned me because access to my children would be limited.

I felt trapped, enclosed, and I needed a way out. I went downstairs to ask to see another apartment. The agent showed me another apartment and gave me a tour of the building. She showed me the facility. I became more relaxed with the thought of staying in a high-rise apartment. However, I wanted to make sure that they moved me to a more updated apartment. I felt uncomfortable staying in my current apartment because of the old furniture. I wondered if this ratty used furniture was what I had to look forward to as a single mother.

The agent told me that I needed to stay in the current apartment for one night and then request another apartment in the morning. During this time, I was speaking to Mr. Swiss about my concerns and fear of being alone and feeling claustrophobic. I cried that night in the apartment with the dilapidated furniture. I needed to change apartments and fast. Mr. Swiss was worried about me, but he was also stressed back home with his new responsibilities of the children. He was in tears knowing that I was away and we were not in a good place.

The next morning, the agent met me to take me to another apartment that was several blocks away. The building was huge. It had several buildings attached to the main building. The size overwhelmed me. When I stepped inside, it was even bigger than the outside. We walked in the building, and two large escalators were leading to the security entrance. It felt like I was in a mall. This building was even larger than the other, and I felt more closed in.

We passed the security gate, the glass door opened and let us into the large three-part building. We went towards the elevator, and I noticed that there was digital wall. There was no number on the top the elevator door or an up or down button front. She said that all I needed was to put the key next to the elevator door and it will send me to the floor associated with the key. The elevator door opened and I walked in.

Again there was no number showing the different floors or the ability to punch the floor number. The walls were padded with gray padding. I felt nervous, unsure of where the elevator was taking me; I felt even more trapped in this environment. I knew this was not the place for me. As we exited the elevator, the apartment was right there in front of the elevator door. This will be super loud.

When we walked in, I noticed that the decor was brand new; there was a large bed with plush white blankets, a plush shaggy blue rug, dark hardwood floors, a small kitchenette with newer appliances and a great view of the city. Yet, I still felt claustrophobic.

I had to get out of there!

As we waited for the elevator I had an anxiety attack knowing that the elevator didn't seem accessible, the building was so large that it felt like a maze. I needed to get out of there. The apartment felt like my relationship, controlled, and restricted.

We went back to the other building. I told her that I would stay there, but in a new apartment. I did not want to feel like I had lost everything: the relationship, my self-respect, dignity, my purpose, and my life. So, she found another apartment, and I felt relieved. It was time for me to start living in this new environment.

I settled in, and the phone rang. It was Mr. Swiss; he needed help with the schedule for one of the girls. I decided to assist him even though he was so agitated and nervous about the complexity of the schedule. He and I both realized that he never dealt with anything at the school, aftercare, or the gymnastics facility. He was clueless about the girls and their life outside of the home. He was aware, but he didn't know how I organized their day-to-day activities. He was a mess. The day-to-day organization of the girls' school clothes, their ballet clothes, their gymnastic outfits, their lunch, breakfast, instruments, play dates, phone numbers of parents, teachers, homework, dinner, bedtime routine completely overwhelmed Mr. Swiss. He realized that he couldn't do this without me and the girls' schedule was a job in itself. So, I assisted him because the household is a business. The next day I woke up and realized that I had no idea what to do. I had no schedule, no plan, no children, no husband, no food, nothing.

I am by myself!

I had to make a plan of how I would utilize these four weeks of clarity. First thing, I decided that I needed to cleanse my body and soul. I needed to go to an acupuncturist because my stomach was still in knots from anxiety. A friend of mine referred me to an old-school Chinese acupuncturist in Chinatown. I got an appointment immediately.

She was stern in her voice, not friendly, but educated in the healing components of acupuncture and holistic medicine. She told me to stick out my tongue, and I did.

She asked me, *"Why are you stifling your emotions?"* I said, *"This is not the first time that I heard this."* She then asked, *"Why are you so angry?"* Here we go with the angry black woman stereotype. But then, I checked myself with the stereotype of her stereotyping me. *"I'm not angry."* She looked at me and said, *"Who are you angry with and why are you so sad? You need to express yourself even if it hurts."* She must be seeing my anger towards Mr. Swiss and my sadness in our relationship.

Why am I so angry?

Then, she placed all these needles outside my body, and I laid there. I felt vulnerable, and it felt good. It felt like a hot massage with no one massaging me. I let myself release my toxic energy and anger. I was naked in my thoughts, and then I farted. My stomach started to release toxic gas from my system. My stomach got super flat. I felt great. I immediately realized that I was holding extreme amounts of toxic energy, gas, and emotions inside my body.

I felt great!

When I got back to the apartment, I wrote down all of the things that I wanted to accomplish during my four weeks. I wanted to find my 'She Power' again.

1) Workout every day in the week.
2) Run on the treadmill for a 7 minute mile.
3) Go for a walk in the city and explore something new each day.

4) Learn something new each day and write about it.
5) Answer the questions: Who am I now? What is my role? What do I want for my life?
6) Look at the things that I like and love outside of my relationship.
7) Embrace every moment.
8) Go out and enjoy myself.
9) Understand what my self-worth is.
10) Understand my WHY in my relationship.

I also needed to answer the question:

What if I had a divorce? Then what?

I wanted to answer these questions without the interference of my friends, my family, or Mr. Swiss renting space in my mind. I avoided or told people that I didn't want to talk. It was too much, and the influence of others was too intense. I wanted to be clear about my thoughts and feelings, so I was silent about fears in my relationship.

Week 2 - The awakening

My friend and I went to a day party. As we left, we were walking; a woman approached us. She was a short Latina woman with long dark hair and a burn mark on her left shoulder. Her voice was raspy. She told my friend and me that she was a psychic and she would love to read us. I looked at my friend while she spoke to us with her raspy voice, and I shouted, *"Let's do it!"* My friend said, *"You're crazy!"* I said, *"Oh well, we only live once. It's only $10. Let's do it! It's funny! Why not?"* My friend, looked at me like I was super crazy but was intrigued by this little raspy-voiced Latina woman. We turned our heads, and she was gone! She disappeared.

SPOOKY!

So, of course, I said, *"Let's call the number and see what she says!"* My friend said, *'Timna you're crazy! I would only do something like this with my sister!"* I said, *"What the hell! Come on!"* She reluctantly agreed and called the number. We got an appointment!

One hour later, after a shot of tequila, we stumbled over to the location and guess who was behind us? The psychic! She appeared and, of course, this spooked us the hell out, but we were tipsy. Even though we were spooked out, we still had a 'Let's do it!' attitude. She walked us over to her office. Of course, her sign was blaring bright above a cigar shop, which had smoke coming from the door. This was definitely a scene taken straight out of the movies.

We went into a building that was a bit dilapidated and spooky. As my friend would always say, **"Should my Gucci bag be here right now?"** The answer was, **"No!"**

It was creepy and cheap, but we still went in. Her Gucci bag and my YSL stayed close to our chest as we walked through the hallway and up the stairs to the apartment where the psychic had her office. As we walked towards the office door, we wondered who was going first. Of course, I went in first. The psychic immediately started to ramble her prediction of the present and future. She told me things that scared me, made me feel good, and made me think. I started to have an ugly cry!

I was a mess! After my session, I knew that I was sad, depressed, and my love for Mr. Swiss was weakened. I knew that he was my roommate, not my soulmate. I could live with him, but I will never have a passionate love for him. It would be my choice to be alone or to be with him. It was my choice. I cried.

Did I want to be with him?

That night he sent me an email.

Mr. Swiss:
It just came to me. We both didn't clearly speak out our feelings when we were in Germany. You might have told me in different ways, but I wasn't receiving it as I wasn't fully aware or on top of things. You told me what you needed me to do when I came home. I didn't explain or admit that I simply couldn't deal with administration work at home as it made me sick to my stomach. I had to translate everything at work for my company. My brain was spinning from the amount of hyperactivity in having to use my brain at work and home. When I came home

every day it was like: Take out the garbage! Do the lawn! Did you call the registration office, the driver's license, the bank accounts, transferring the money, the kids' registration at the Swiss consulate? I really want my car! Why can't you get the car registered? Why do you not care for me? It was more an explanation of what I need to do or why I am not doing things for you.

My issue at that time:

Me talking High German all day that wasn't my home language and coming home to speak English. Me having to translate administrative, legal paper on words I have never heard of. My company expectation of me to know how to do this or better, **I thought they expected me to know how to do it** (I judged the situation). I was completely overwhelmed by the pressure at work and at home, but I told you that I was fine. But then in your eyes "Why can I not take care of you and the little things you asked?"

I failed to express my feelings on what I am going through to you and specifically to my boss.

And on top of it, you didn't tell me how you felt. Or better, how bad it really made you feel. It was more of telling vs me knowing how awful you felt. I learned about how you felt at a later point, but it was too late. It wasn't like I was aware either so you may have told me in different ways, but it wasn't clear to me.

I was a coward as I thought it would show weakness! I just woke up and realized my fear was that I am being exposed, to be perceived as weak and incompetent. My fear was so big that I completely ignored my feeling and brainwashed myself that I am fine. So, I shut down and didn't say anything and put the pressure on me that I just needed to do it on my own. Which I wasn't able to in a way that you felt like I am truly taking care of you. I didn't know that it eventually will break me down because I didn't ask for help. I couldn't bear the pressure from myself, you and work and that's why I looked for an escape in gaming/gambling.

Now I just realized this lesson...

You told me to write down my thoughts I wake up with. Well... This is what I thought in my sleep prior to me waking up. It was a dream I woke up with and I was like. Wow!

I am super sorry for my inability to admit my weakness as well to not being able to tell you what I was going through at work and home.

We both had an awakening that week. We talked about the past in great detail and the resentment we had for each other during our time in Germany. We became naked with each other about the past, but it was still not okay. I still felt sick talking to him and he still was crying every time we spoke. We were both a mess. However, in the mess, we had an opportunity to listen about the past and understand our core issues of lack of trust, respect, love and commitment. We talked about how our relationship become fake and the love we once had for each that had evaporated in time. The resentment from the past overshadowed the present and the future.

How do we move forward from the past into the future?

Week 3 - The Divorce

That week I still felt anger towards Mr. Swiss. I was tired of his sweet nothings. I felt like he was manipulating me with his words and his lack of truly saying he was sorry. I couldn't deal with him. He wrote me many emails and sent me numerous texts. He asked me why I wasn't truly telling him how I felt about him and the relationship. He was looking for a sense of me loving him, but I could not give him that. He felt like a pest, pestering me each day and each night. I couldn't breathe. We texted back and forth discussing what our lives would be like separated from one another. We had a plan after my return that he would leave for four weeks to find his own clarity. I thought he was serious about finding himself, but he was more interested in understanding what my plans would be.

He texted me asking me questions and badgering me about my individual accounts and how much money I had saved. He wanted to know if I had the financial freedom to leave, but I didn't. I didn't have enough money to survive without him. He knew that he had financial control over me. I felt trapped once again and defeated.

Mr. Swiss:
I was wondering, your mom always told you to save for a rainy day so, how much money have you saved? I see that you have transfer $500 in your personal account every month for the last 3 years.

Me:
Are you worried about $500 a month? We pay our housekeeper or driver more than that? Am I worth less than our help around the house?

Mr. Swiss:
No I didn't mean that, I was just wondering how much money you have in your account?

I did not respond. I just sat in my apartment and started to weep. I cried out loud asking God why didn't I save more money and why did my husband think I was his slave. How dare he ask me about $500 a month? Was he crazy! This was emotional abuse! He was f*cking with my head and I was pissed!

Mr. Swiss then called the apartment phone and I didn't answer. I was crying out loud in fear of not having money. I couldn't control my anger, my shame, my lack of financial gain in the relationship. I cried and cried.

Why me?!

Mr. Swiss just kept on calling. I decided to pick up after the fifth call.

Me (weeping), *"Yes?"*

Mr. Swiss said, *"I'm sorry that I hit a nerve, but I was wondering about this money. I'm sorry that I made you feel this way, but I sent you an email detailing what you can have financially if we divorce. I will take care of you and the kids. I'm sorry."* Me, weeping, *"You're evil, and I don't want anything! I'm done! F*ck you! I will go on welfare if I need to. I have my education, my degrees, and my God given talent of getting a job. So, I'm not afraid anymore and your sorry doesn't mean anything to me. Don't talk to me and send me the paperwork from the lawyers. I'm done!"* I hung up. He called back.

Mr. Swiss then stated to me, *"The law in the state of Georgia will not give you alimony because you had an affair and that gambling was not considered betrayal in the eyes of the law."* I later found out that this was not true. He went on to say that he wanted the kids to be secure, but felt the need to write up a financial agreement which he then emailed to me. I saw this has a stress tactic. I could not forgive him and I questioned if I could ever fall in love with him again. Then his email came:

Mr. Swiss
Please read this as it is my truth!

When my parents had a divorce, I went from rich to poor. My dad f*cked my mom over. I experienced how my mom scrambled for work. Hustled for us. Scrambling for us to have a roof and food, as well the freedom of being a child. One night, we almost had to sleep in the car, but she found a friend that would take us in. (Long story I tell you later)

I wrote the whole email below and when I was finished, I realized that I went from riches of having a beautiful home to moving into an apartment and downgrading to another apartment and moving again. I don't want that for our children!!!

Please read on...

We're on a roller coaster. All the issues will come up, and we have to resolve them if we have any chance to survive this individually and as friends and potentially as a couple.

I had no idea how deeply you felt about the money. This can't be going on forward. I looked at the joint accounts as a symbol of me giving you everything. But you look at it of me controlling your spending.. I am sorry. That's not what I want and this can be easily fixed in several different ways.

The email continues...

Last, since I went through an ugly divorce of my parents as a child, it is my true feeling that I want to make sure you know you and the kids are taken care of, even if it means we will not be together. I am happy to sign an agreement that no matter what; I will be responsible to pay you x amount. This could be a monthly fee for x month or whatever. There are creative ways to create a lucrative deal for you for years after. If you have no income you get x. If you make x you get x etc. The deal should be crafted to mainly benefit you. I am ok with you holding the stick with the carrot. Honestly...

Currently, you feel treated unfairly and underpaid. I want to make sure you know when I say, all my money is your money and I am ok for you to have the controls. And if things would come to a new beginning for each of us, I want to make sure you know that you are walking away secured with the ability to provide for the kids as well keep your status quo. Hopefully it will never come to it, but I want to free you from this feeling of me holding you back through a financial disadvantage. The reason I am doing this? I then will know that you are staying because of me and not for the money. And if you leave, you always have the right to adjust the deal to make it equally fair and not just benefiting you. You will have the sole ownership on how things are being split out fairly. I trust that you will not screw me over.

You said it on Sunday. We will go through a roller coaster of emotions. I am truly sorry if I made you feel like shit. That was not what I intended at all.

Thanks

We talked everyday knowing that the end was near. I felt free! However, I wondered if he was still manipulating me and if his email was just words to get me back. Would he actually follow through with his promises about finances?

A few days passed and then there was another email.

Mr. Swiss:

In this week, I keep telling Anavi and specifically Ivy their sorry doesn't mean nothing if you don't change. Every single time I tell them, No you're not sorry if keep on doing it!

I know that I have been wrong. I have not supported you. I have given excuses. I have told you sorry. But I haven't truly changed until you left. So yes, I understand now by being with the kids that sorry didn't mean anything.

I can't promise you anything. As I have promised too many times and simply disappointed. I was living in a bubble of thoughts that didn't allow me to live the life I deep down longed for. I know that just from this week with the kids, I never felt more connected to life than in the last two weeks. I have a purpose. And yes, I clearly didn't have a real purpose prior to starting with Tai Chi. I had fake purposes, like I need to make more money and I need to provide. I need... I need... I need...

My purpose is to live life, to experience it with my soul to see how many people I can touch on a daily basis.

It's not about you or the kids. It's everybody and everything around me. Our dog, Mr Wrinkle's changes with me. He is a reflection of my soul.

I always thought I used to be intuitive (even yesterday morning when you talked to me), I finally decided to look up this word. Nope, not me... I might have been when I was a child but over time my soul changed. Yes, a soul can change (looked that up too); my assumption was it can't change.

Anyways; I am not intuitive and yes, I don't believe in symbols. I instead believe in the power of energy (I know this because I am really good in sales) and I am superstitious. I didn't really know that or wanted to admit that but every time I see a symbol or hear a bad comment I touch wood or I imagine to touch wood. It always allowed me to override what people otherwise would think of a ginks. And it has worked for me on trusting in my power of energy.

My issue I had is that I tried to use my energy wrongly with you, just like in sales, manipulating the outcomes of everything to get something. In life, we don't need to get anything. We need to only give.

It's something I never understood.

I have to give to myself by giving myself to me and others. What you're getting in return is fulfillment. Something I have learned by being with the kids and Mr. Wrinkles. There is nothing I expect from them in return, but I am truly happy to be in this position to being there for them.

I cleaned the house yesterday morning and I thought sincerely of no longer using the cleaning crew. At least not every two weeks. It's healing to clean as it helped me appreciate what we have and to touch it. But then I also looked at the things I couldn't get done and I noticed that if doing this all the time by yourself, it will no longer be an act of awareness rather a routine and can become overwhelming. That is what you felt because you had no help. Something else I learned this week.

I'm not good yet at expressing as I never was truly aware, that is why I am writing you. I'm changing for the first time since I was 19. That was the time I stopped playing soccer and went into my business with my partner. I ran away from my passion or from my soul out of fear of failure and never forgave myself for it. I went into a depression privately, but faked it externally, because people respected me. I felt like it was right. I gave up on being truthful to myself.

I was truthful when I left Switzerland as I went against everyone and also against my friend's advice. That's the first time I did something after 4 years that was in my heart. Going to the US was like me walking into the Tai Chi place. Why Miami and how the heck did I end up in Tampa? I let my soul guide me on both.

No need to tell you our story...

This all is still very new; it's now 4 weeks since California... Only 3 weeks since you asked for a separation.

I am a baby learning how to walk; literally. My Tai Chi teacher just told me that I now know how to walk forward, still need practice on the kick walk but you get my point.

It's a scary thing to do, specifically as I don't have anyone here. I have no mentor, advisor, true friend on where I built up the trust of being truthful at all times. My walk is by myself. And I accepted that. My friend who is now my boss knows me more than anyone but she is my boss now. I opened up to her as I missed to do it with my old boss when I was Germany.

So I just started the process. I'm innocently trusting this new path as I have been doing with my job. I never was aiming to get promoted, I never knew what will happen in a year. I simply did my job with enjoyment and passion and made that other connection, touched that other person and made that next sale. It was a day to day vision. I trusted that it will all come out ok by just doing.

I'm just doing now in my personal life day by day, step by step. I can't promise you anything. Tai Chi's first lesson: you have to slow down to the slow motion of the movement to experience that one single motion with everything that goes with it. The smell, the breathing, the muscular pain, the emotion. The Tai Chi has seen me change as I have seen me change. It's just a simple step but it means everything. I have ignored all my steps. I am learning to experience.

I woke up with no thought, no dream. Wasn't thinking about what I will write. It's raw from my soul as I did not make any correction to the flow other than spell check.

Hmmm... He is a good writer. Is he sorry now? Will he change and implement thoughts into action when I return? His words are like poetry, but his heart is like stone when he is around me. What should I do? Should I stay or leave?

Week 4 - The Renewal

I woke up and knew that it was the home stretch, I had one more week. What will happen? I'm a new woman with a new outlook on life.
- I went to the movies by myself
- I went to dinner by myself
- I went to breakfast by myself
- I was physically fit
- I cooked by myself
- I explored; I wrote; I dreamed; I danced; I laughed all by myself
- I lived by myself for the first time in 20 years
- I went to a Broadway play by myself
- My stomach pains went away
- I loved myself
- I felt free
- I was renewed

The Question...

Do I want to go back to my life as it was or do I want to make a change to be by myself with my girls? What should I do for my last week? Where should I go? Who am I now? I want a tattoo!

I told Mr. Swiss and he said, *"I'm disappointed in you. Why would you want to get a tattoo? Why would you do this without me?"* That's why I'm going because I don't want to ask him for anything. I'm taking action for myself and this is something that I want to do. I'm a grown woman. If he loves me, he will respect my decision. F*ck him!

I told Mr. Swiss, *"I know that you have a problem with me getting a tattoo alone without you, but this is my body. I'm finally doing something for myself. Please respect my decision. I will send you a picture when it's done. Thanks for your support!"* He then realized that I didn't need him to make a life decision. I was jumping into the water by myself naked and free without judgment or approval from him. I was FREE.

I got a tattoo!

After receiving the tattoo, I was walking back to the apartment and a young beautiful Middle Eastern woman stopped me on the street. She was pushing a baby carriage, while walking alongside her husband.

She said, *"You must think I'm crazy, but I felt your energy. I was walking, and I sense an intense energy. I wondered who it was and I couldn't figure it out. I just thought that it was so strong. As soon as you came across the street, I knew it was you."* As she was talking, I then clinched my purse because I'm a New Yorker and a stranger was talking to me. Despite my apprehension, I leaned in and continued to listen to her message. Her voice matched her appearance, cute, innocent, caring, and petite.

The young woman said, *"I have a message; He doesn't know how to love you. He doesn't know how to show love. His actions are different from his words. Forgive him. Forgive him; he knows not how to love you."* I looked at her, realized what she had told me and immediately started to tear up. I thanked her for the message.

I then ran into the apartment building, went straight to the security guard to tell her what just happened. Talking to the security guard was something that I did every night when I entered the building. I was shocked, scared, and confused about the message but I knew what I had to do. After having my nightly wrap up with the security guard, I took the elevator upstairs to call Mr. Swiss. I told him, *"I forgive you. I forgive you. I understand now. I need you to love me and I will show you how. I can't promise that we'll be together forever, but all I know is that we need to figure this shit out. This is an unhealthy relationship! We need help! I will try to work this out.*

One question remained to be answered. Yet, only time would tell.

Should I stay?
or
Should I leave?